how to start a home-based

Consulting Business

how to start a home-based

Consulting Business

Bert Holtje

gpp®

Guilford, Connecticut

For my son, Jim Holtje, also an author. As he freely admits, he's a chip off the old writer's block.

Library of Congress Cataloging-in-Publication Data
Holtje, Herbert.
 How to start a home-based consulting business : define your specialty, build a client base, make yourself indispensable, create a fee structure, find trusted subcontractors and specialists, become a sought-after expert / Bert Holtje.
    p. cm. — (Home-based business series)
 Includes index.
 ISBN 978-0-7627-5265-2
1. Business consultants. 2. Home-based businesses. I. Title.
 HD69.C6H616 2010
 001—dc22

                             2009029497

Printed in the United States of America
10 9 8 7 6 5 4 3 2 1

Contents

Introduction

Many people become consultants by accident, without ever planning for it. The chief engineer of a manufacturing company discovers that he has become the go-to guy when his colleagues need his special advice. After a while, it dawns on him that he can charge others for his advice, but he can't do it while collecting a salary from an employer, so he takes the plunge. The accountant who sees that her employer pays outsiders a lot more money for work that she does as an employee decides to leave and hang out her own shingle.

Few people, other than those who take jobs at consulting firms right out of school, think about consulting work right from the start. Some fall into it. Some plan for it after a few years of working for others. And some discover it when their employers outsource their jobs to places you can't find on any map.

As talented and experienced as some people may be, few really have a clue about starting a business of their own. And even fewer realize that most of the major expenses involved in starting and running a consultancy are really unnecessary, especially those that involve having an office anywhere but in your own home.

Suggest to someone who is thinking about consulting that he or she should consider working from a home office, and you will probably be laughed at. However, in the pages that follow you will meet some highly successful consultants who have always worked from home offices. One consults regularly from a New York apartment with heads of state in many major Latin American countries. Another, a human resources consultant who counts Fortune 500 companies among his clients, lives in the middle of America's historic past just a stone's throw from the Delaware River. You will also meet consultants whose careers may be less glamorous, but whose incomes are just as enviable. They all agree on one thing: Working from a home office is the only way to go.

Just for the record, I have worked from a home office for the last thirty-eight years and have no plans to do anything differently for the next thirty-eight. My home and office is the penthouse of a historic building in a small town on the west shore of the Hudson River.

At one time or another all of us thought we needed something more impressive than a home office. It was an ego thing. After all—who would trust a consultant who works from home? The answer is that none of my clients and none of the clients of the people you will meet in these pages care where we live. None has ever asked, and few of us have ever invited clients to visit our home offices. Working from a home office is not an issue. The most important thing is being able to provide the services your clients need.

That being said, there are some special issues in working from home, apart from keeping your dog from barking when you are on the phone with a client in London. Your home office must function just as one would in an office building, which means that you have to adjust your plans accordingly. It means that you'd better be aware of the laws your town may have enacted about home businesses. And it means that your neighbors might get a little annoyed by the number of times a day the FedEx truck blocks their driveway while making deliveries to you.

If you are just getting started you will need to write a business plan, even if you are starting without borrowed capital. The tax implications for a home business are different than those for an office rented in an office building. Those who have yet to look deeply into the matter are initially thrilled that they might be able to write off some significant expenses by working from home. However, if you ever sell the home that houses you and your business, you just might be hit with some taxes that you never planned for (more about that later).

Far too many home-based consultants commingle their business money with their personal money when they're getting started. What should be a pretty simple tax return for most home-based consultants can turn into a nightmare when it comes time to separate the piles of invoices, bills, checks, and possibly even cash that the local, state, and federal governments want to tax. (You'll see what I mean when you read chapter 8.)

Just in case you never get to chapter 6 (What Are You Worth?), let me warn you never to reduce your fees just because you work from home. And don't be afraid to send reminders to those whose payments are overdue. Chapter 7 (Managing the Money You Make) explains why overdue payments not only drain your operating capital, but also set a bad precedent for both current and future clients.

Every home-based consultant has to establish both an operating network and a support network. You will meet people from all over the country who can help you, along with plenty who can waste your time. Internet networks have made it possible for home-based consultants to help others and to also be helped, with everything from daily problems to major issues. But it has also made it possible for those with some time on their hands to impose on those who are trying to finish a client report at midnight. The consultants I will introduce to you in these pages have some interesting things to say about helping others, being helped, and flat-out wasting time.

Then, of course, there may come a time when you'll become so well known as a consultant in your field that larger firms will want you to join them, or companies you have consulted with will offer you money and titles that make you and your home-based consultancy seem puny by comparison. Should you take the offer? If you decide to stay put, will the larger consultancy move in on your business? Will the company that offers you the VP title and the reserved parking spot dump you once you have solved all of their problems for them? These are real issues, and although you are just beginning to think about becoming a consultant, you should include them in your planning. Chapter 12 is the place to look for the answers to these and other growth-related issues.

Now, let's get you started on your consulting career!

Why Do It? Why Not?

If I may be permitted to begin with a cliché, a consultant is someone who borrows your watch to tell you the time. Those who like to drop this bit of condescension on their consultant friends seldom stop to think that perhaps the person from whom the watch was borrowed couldn't tell time. In any case, being a consultant is like being a viola player—you will be both admired and teased. But as a consultant, you will probably make more money than many of your friends who toil at jobs that don't make them especially happy. And if you work from a home office, you have no commuting expenses. Oh, and yes, I do occasionally borrow a client's watch, but I always return it with the correct time!

Not unlike many home-based businesses, consulting requires some special and marketable talents, as well as personal characteristics that are not at all like the characteristics needed to make it as someone's employee. In fact, most of the people who give consulting a try usually return to the corporate fold—not for lack of ability, but because they totally underestimated what it takes to build their own business.

There are more than a few good books in print on how to start and run a consulting business. Most, however, only take a superficial whack at the advantages and problems of working from home; and I'm not aware of any that address the business from the point of view of sharing a home with a spouse and maybe a few kids—and possibly a report-eating dog.

Today's Consultant

Consultants today have many options—from being an expert advisor to working hand in hand with clients on a day-to-day basis. Whether they just advise or actually pitch in, consultants work in virtually every field of business, as well as government and nongovernmental organizations. They also work for private charities, social service organizations, and nonprofit foundations. While you will find some home-based consultants who work only with local clients, you are just as likely to find others whose clients include heads of state around the world. In short, it's a wide—and wide-open—field.

Whether a consultant is helping a monarch in a small country to establish a fiscal policy, or another is helping a small, local manufacturer to implement a shop-floor management system, the basic work has a lot in common. So, if I use an example from an international consultant, don't think that the underlying principles won't apply to your local work. They will.

Between 1980 and 1990, the consulting field grew by more than 20 percent. At the beginning of the twenty-first century, the field actually shrank a little, and up until the current economic turndown, it had been slowly growing again. Now, however, it's a good bet that the field will expand greatly. So, it's a good time to think about consulting, and especially about establishing a home-based consultancy. In 2007, a good economic year, global revenues from management consulting exceeded $300 billion. Since consultants are hired more often in bad times than in good, you can only imagine what the potential might be.

Growth Potential

Small, home-based consultancies are by necessity niche-focused businesses. However, more than a few of the large multiclient and multidiscipline consulting firms that exist today were started by one individual with a single focus, and originally run from home-based offices. More and more consulting firms are working with nonbusiness organizations than ever before. Also on the plus side, many of the large, broad-based firms that got their start in accounting have been closing their non-accounting specialty operations, mainly to comply with federal regulations. All in all, the picture looks good for you if you have a specialty that is in demand; the credentials to attract attention; and the option of keeping your overhead down by working from a home office.

You can probably help clients with your special advice as well as provide them with some hands-on help. In other words, you can provide prescriptive service when only advice is needed, and process-based consulting when hands-on help is needed. Most new consultants offer both of these services as solo practitioners, later specializing in one or the other. And, if they get big enough to employ enough people, they will again separate the services they provide. For now, as a home-based consultant (and probably a solo practitioner), you will be doing both. This brings me to the core issue of this chapter: assessing your interests, abilities, and goals, as well as the potential market or markets that are available to you.

Who Are You, What Can You Do, and Who Needs Your Services?

Before I get into the specific issues of consulting, let's look at the personal factors involved in what it takes to start and run your own business. I'll talk about the legal and financial issues later; for now, some soul-searching and self-analysis is required. For that, I have enlisted the aid of an expert on the subject, Marc Dorio.

I asked Marc to tell me what he considered to be the most important personal characteristics necessary to start a consulting business—especially for those who are planning to operate from a home-based office. These are the elements he feels are critical for success:

- A willingness to take calculated risks
- An understanding that nothing is certain, but that with the right attitude, uncertainty can be held to a minimum (even if seldom eliminated)
- A willingness to work hard, even when there is only a small initial return on the effort

Meet Marc Dorio

Marc Dorio is a home-based management consultant who specializes in management development and corporate human resource consulting. With more than twenty-five years' experience and graduate degrees in organizational psychology, Marc includes Fortune 500 and Fortune 100 companies on his client list. He is the author of *The Personnel Manager's Desk Book, The Staffing Problem Solver, The Complete Idiot's Guide to the Perfect Interview, The Complete Idiot's Guide to Getting the Job You Want,* and *The Complete Idiot's Guide to Career Advancement.* Marc teaches college courses, and appears frequently as a guest on national TV shows—all of this while working from a home office in historic western New Jersey, in clear view of the Delaware River.

- A view of change as challenge, not as something to avoid
- A sense of personal as well as business organization
- An ability to plan ahead and an understanding that all plans are tentative
- A realistic view of life and of the world of work
- An understanding as well as an appreciation of the power of language and numbers
- An ability to work from home without having to apologize for it
- A sense of professionalism that transcends the location of your business

Marc explains that whether you are the go-to expert in your consulting role or are servicing clients in a facilitative role, you must see yourself in the foreground of the work situation. If you are at all apologetic about working from a home office, your clients will sense it, and it will become difficult to take on and maintain the consultant's leadership role. As he puts it quite succinctly, "If you are not comfortable in your own skin, you will find it difficult to convince clients that your ideas are workable, or that you will be able to do the things you were engaged to do. A simple thing like being apologetic about a home office can sink you with a client before you ever get started."

Marc works with many companies that have internal consulting groups, but he says that rather than seeing them as competitors, start-up consultants should view these internal consulting groups as better sources of consulting engagements than many other companies. "The reason for this," he explains, "is that consultants new to the field are boutiques. That is, they are small, narrowly focused, and flexible in their approach to problems a client may be facing. Also, those who manage internal consulting operations seldom feel threatened by smaller firms. The small firms are task-oriented. The huge consulting firms may do an excellent job, but once in the door, they are immediately looking for other assignments in all or most of the areas in which they consult."

In order to develop a successful consulting business, it's essential to be able to work with many different clients of varying temperament. Marc explains that it is often easier to work with internal consultants than it is with others in the client firm. "A consultant brought in to solve a major sales problem who has to report to the client's sales manager is not going to have an easy time of it," he says. "However, when you are engaged by an internal consultant, you have a buffer between you and the person who is probably going to resent you if he or she is forced to work with you directly." He points out that beginning consultants should jump at the chance to take assignments from internal consulting departments of large organizations, and should not feel intimidated by the size of the company.

Personality Traits That Make the Difference

Consultants, whether they are doing process work or prescriptive work for their clients, are first and foremost problem solvers. If the client didn't have a problem and just needed someone to do a job, the company would either take on a full-time employee or work with temps to get a particular job done. Always keep that in mind, especially when you run into resentment among the ranks of client employees.

You might consider taking any number of tests to see how well you would fit into the role of independent consultant. Marc Dorio continues to use most of them, but he says, "As a psychologist, I can usually spot certain characteristics that stand out. However, it's not easy for anyone to look at themselves without all the biases that a lifetime has left us with. The average blowhard, for example, is totally unaware of just how obnoxious he is. Some of the brightest people I have met in my work have been quiet and unassuming. While they often have the best ideas, unfortunately, they usually don't push hard enough to implement them."

I asked Marc to provide some guidelines for potential consultants to use in order to get a realistic idea of his or her chances for success. He offers the following suggestions, but notes that if the individual has any serious doubts, it's really best to take some of the professional career tests that are available.

"A consultant must be able to pick the right problem-solving technique to fit the client and the problem," Marc explains. "It's a mistake to think that one problem-solving approach will work in every situation. And the consultant must be flexible enough to be able to adapt to both the client and the best problem-solving orientation."

What's Needed to Succeed as a Consultant

It's a mistake to think of yourself in either/or terms when you are trying to see whether or not you might be suited to consulting work. Unfortunately, many of the popular personality tests give the impression that you are either an introvert or an extrovert. Very few people could be classified as fully one type or another, and if you run into any who come close, they are usually not all that pleasant to be around. Rather, people tend to be outgoing in some situations and less expressive in others.

This is simply an adaptive mechanism at work, so don't be concerned if you consider yourself a "thinker" and sometimes prefer not to be the center of attention. The most successful consultants adapt themselves to the assignment at hand and the people with whom they work. I asked Marc to give me examples of how introverts and extroverts would address typical consulting situations. You can probably see something of both categories in yourself.

Introverts

Introverts seldom act impulsively. When addressing a consulting issue, they usually look for the internal logic of the situation. They want to see how things hang together, relate to each other, and influence each other before even thinking about a possible solution. Many extroverted clients see this kind of reflection as a waste of time. When dealing with a client like this, you have to be patient; instead of challenging his way of thinking, show him what you are doing and why you are doing it. This requires considerable fortitude in some cases, especially when the client has engaged you on an hourly basis.

Introverts look for internal logic when working on a problem. They are less likely to "think out loud" in brainstorming sessions. They will spend more time reflecting on the issues than will those who prefer to throw the problem on the table and kick it around directly. They want their ideas to be internally consistent before they discuss them. Simply put, those who prefer quiet contemplation before expressing any ideas are:

- Reflective
- Inner-directed
- More logical than those who are more outer-directed

Marc Dorio's tip . . .

It's a mistake to think of quiet people as being less capable than those who are gregarious and outgoing. Quiet people are not antisocial, although they may be perceived so by people who are very outgoing. Most quiet people simply dislike small talk. A less outgoing person working as a consultant often gains more information on a client's project than might one who feels a need to talk constantly. I would definitely say that quiet people have a strong advantage in consulting situations.

Extroverts

Extroverts tend to be somewhat more impulsive than introverts. In the extreme, they consider those who prefer to think through a problem more carefully to be wasting time. They think of themselves as being more real-world-oriented than those whose first inclinations are to look for some internal consistency first. Extroverts will usually suggest group brainstorming sessions rather than having individual team members think through an issue and return with written reports. Extroverts are more likely to listen to what others in the group have to say than might those who are more inner-directed.

Extroverts usually prefer drawing on personal experience rather than considering research results. Seldom do they downplay research completely, but when the results of a research study dramatically contradict a closely held belief, extroverts tend to ignore the data, or at least try to soften it. This is not always a problem, however. Research, when tempered with well-articulated, real-world experience, is often more productive than sticking slavishly to data because "the numbers can't possibly be wrong." Extroverts, then, are:

- Reality-oriented
- Outer-directed
- More likely to listen to others than those who are more internally driven

It should be obvious that success in consulting is based more on flexibility and adaptability than on identifying yourself as either an introvert or an extrovert. If you can play both roles in the appropriate situations, you will be well on your way toward becoming a successful consultant.

Judgment

Many consulting assignments will not call for you to tell the client exactly what to do; rather, they will require you to provide the client with your best judgment as to what can be done to solve the problem. This often involves offering alternative suggestions and scenarios for success, based on your perceptions of what the client will want. How you arrive at the suggestions you provide your clients—demonstrating your own judgment—is critical for success in the business. Just presenting a laundry list of ideas is not the way to go.

If you have associates, you can bounce your ideas off of them. However, if you are working alone, you will have to establish a system by which you evaluate the alternatives you're willing to give a client. Looking back on how well a similar idea worked in a similar situation is an excellent way to make a judgment. If you can break the problem down, step by step, the pitfalls and benefits will usually show up clearly. It's when you have a few possibilities of equal value that your ability to make sound judgments comes into play.

Sound judgment is a blend of reality and fantasy. If you prefer to make snap decisions, consulting may not be the right field for you. If you prefer to think problems through carefully and review your impressions based on what has worked in the past, and what is most likely to work in a current assignment, you fit the profile of a successful consultant. This is not to say that your snap decision might not be the right one, but well-reasoned judgments are far more likely to be workable. Sound judgment is most likely a factor of:

- A clear understanding of the problem, and what has—and hasn't—worked in the past
- A willingness to challenge your own and others' assumptions
- A command of the facts along with an awareness that other factors may exist that you haven't discovered yet

One of the best ways to test your judgment skills is to ask others for their views of your abilities. Be sure to tell those you ask that whatever they say will not be considered offensive, and that you are looking to evaluate your judgment. Marc Dorio explains, "An informal setting in which you 'talk out loud' and your colleague evaluates your judgment of a particular problem is an especially good way to not only get a sense of your abilities, but also to pick up some good advice and practical tips." He also points out that this approach is better taken with only one or two people. "If this is done with a large group," he says, "everyone feels compelled to say something, whether it's relevant or not. This just isn't a helpful situation."

Employment History That Makes a Difference

The first thing people think of when they hear the word *consultant* is someone who works for one of the major management consultant firms. It's understandable. These firms and the people who work for them are in the news all the time. However, there are people in almost every profession who spend their time solving problems you never thought of for companies (or even individuals) you've never heard of.

Years ago I met a couple on the beach of a small island off the coast of Massachusetts. As consultants to craft store owners, they were visiting clients and sampling the island's pleasures. Not a bad way to make a living!

This couple told me that they'd had their own craft store for years and had been quite successful—so much so that they were featured a few years ago in a magazine that circulates to other craft store owners. "We couldn't believe how many letters and calls we got from that article," the husband told me. His wife added, "We began to realize that what we had learned and put to use over the years for ourselves was helpful to others facing similar situations. As much as we liked the business we had started and run for so long, the demanding hours got tougher as time went on. So we thought we'd see if there might be a need for consultants in the field."

They did their homework and found that there were all sorts of consultants serving the retail trade, which included the owners of craft stores. However, they discovered that all the stores served by these consultants sold mainly mass-produced merchandise, while their store sold mainly one-of-a-kind handicrafts. Although they shared many of the same problems, they also had some problems that were unique to their type of craft store. They had found a "niche market," and because they had a history of success that had been well documented by the magazine article, their business pretty much launched itself.

Although we promised to stay in touch, we never did. Years later, however, while vacationing on another island (in the Caribbean this time), I spotted a copy of the craft magazine that had featured the couple. With the store owner's permission, I thumbed through its pages and saw that the couple was now writing a regular advice column for the magazine. Their byline indicated that they had turned their nascent consultancy into a very successful venture.

What this couple did is not all that unusual. They had been there and done that, and were now drawing on their work experience to do what they loved in a different way. I have no way of knowing whether they were making more or less money than they did when they'd had their own store, but they were still at it several years later, so it must have been worthwhile.

Degrees, Diplomas, Certificates, and Other Signs of Achievement

Visit your doctor's office and you'll find that her walls are plastered with framed diplomas and certificates. Just seeing a wall full of such impressive pieces of parchment is enough to establish a comfort zone when you face challenging medical procedures. Nevertheless, when was the last time you read any of them? Like most people, you assume that these certificates and diplomas guarantee some level of quality in the service you are seeking.

It's no different with consultants. Anyone who considers paying you for advice or professional services will expect that you are qualified to do what you say you can do. Your consulting may not require a degree or diploma, but most people will expect you to present something that will attest to your having met some level of qualification.

Case in Point

Peter Drucker, a major force in management theory and one of the most highly regarded consultants of his time, lacked any of the formal credentials considered essential to success in management consulting. Yet, he is considered to have been one of the most productive end enlightened contributors to management theory and practice. Everything he knew he learned from practical, hands-on experience. His work is at the core of many management programs in prestigious graduate schools around the world. He received his honorary degrees long after he had made his name in the industry.

Most fields in which consulting work is done are served by at least one professional organization which accepts members only after they have proven themselves in one way or another. The more-common way of attaining certification is either by taking some sort of pre-membership test, or by completing a course of training offered by the organization or by an affiliated school. Many of the building and construction trade associations offer this kind of certification. Community colleges that do not offer baccalaureate degrees offer certificates of completion in fields in which many people work as consultants. There are even schools and universities which offer distance-learning programs that lead to some form of certification.

And, of course, you can still make it as a consultant without any formal certificates hanging on your wall; that is, if you can show prospective clients that your work experience qualifies you to do the job. The couple I met on that Nantucket beach had no certificates to prove that they were qualified to do what they were doing. However, their success at running a craft store of their own was given an implicit stamp of approval by having been featured in the magazine read by those who could most benefit from their help and experience.

But Is This the Right Field for You?

Maybe you've spent most of your life working in a field that you'd prefer to escape. Ten years as an accountant may be the limit of your endurance. What do you do with a degree or certificate in accounting if you decide you'd like to be a consultant in another field? Surprisingly, many of the major consulting firms can trace their roots to initial work providing simply accounting services. Little by little, or quite rapidly in some cases, these firms branched into general management consulting and then began divisions that focused on some pretty specialized consulting specialties.

It's not always easy to see what else you might be able to do as a consultant when your major work experience has had a fairly narrow focus. One of the best ways to come up with ideas, however, is to work backwards—start from where you want to be and think your way back to where you might be now.

A friend who had solid academic and professional credentials in engineering told me a number of years ago that he did not want to spend the rest of his life with a slide rule (it was that far back). He was an outgoing guy, so I casually suggested that he might consider getting into selling engineered products (with his outgoing personality and professional skills, he was a natural).

He took my advice and moved from the engineering department of the company that employed him to the sales department. It meant a reduction in pay while he got on his feet as a salesperson, but he soon blossomed. He saw that the opportunities were even greater in technical sales consulting, so he left to start his own consulting business. He blossomed there, too. Now retired, he spends his time restoring antique motorcycles and offering free consulting to firms who can benefit from his years of experience.

He is not unusual; more than a few people have gone this route, and many have gone similar routes without the benefit of the credentials he started with. It's a matter of discovering where you want to be, plotting a path to get there, and taking the appropriate steps.

Many skills and abilities are transferable, even though it's not always obvious how they can be used in other fields. However, you might be surprised by what can be done with some fairly well-defined skills and abilities in other fields. One of the best ways to get a handle on where you might be able to use your skills is to take one of the many tests that identify your personal strengths and weaknesses.

Here are just a few of the skills that are immediately transferable from one field to another. Whether you are consulting on engineering problems or employee management issues, these skills can be used anywhere:

- The ability to express thoughts and ideas clearly, both verbally and in writing
- The ability to listen attentively, analyze what you hear, and provide appropriate feedback
- The ability to negotiate issues and mediate when others have differing views
- The ability to identify problems and alternative solutions to these problems
- A sensitivity to what is being said as well as what remains unsaid
- An ability to set realistic goals for yourself as well as for your clients

Avoid the pop tests you so often see in newspapers and magazines. Most community colleges, colleges and universities, and grad schools offer this kind of testing for a fee to people who are not enrolled in their programs. Check with the schools nearest you and see what you can discover.

1. *How can I enter an already-crowded field if I have never worked as a consultant?*

   The best way to get started as a consultant, whether or not you have considerable consulting experience, and regardless of whether the field is already crowded, is to seek a niche with which you are comfortable and make a name there first. It's important to identify a market that is accessible to you. Whether or not you have worked as a consultant is usually less important than having hands-on experience in the relevant field. It's just as easy to convince a potential client that you can solve her problem when you have done it as someone else's employee, and can point to real-world successes. It's the problem-solving history that really counts.

2. *What about first working for another consultant?*

   This is an excellent way to get started in consulting. Many small (and large) consulting firms work with a number of associates who usually work from their own home offices. In fact, it's an excellent way to do consulting work without actually starting your own consulting firm. However, even though you may be associated with someone else, you should do whatever is necessary to protect yourself, both personally and financially. This usually involves either incorporating or setting up as a limited liability corporation (LLC), discussed further in chapter 9.

Chances are that you've been thinking about starting your own home-based consulting business for quite a while. If you are like most people, the positive images you have in your head are those of not having to commute to a dingy office every day and never having to face a cranky boss again. And, of course, your visions include what you will do with all the free time you will have when you open your own business and what you will do with all the money that pours in. We may even meet on an island beach somewhere!

Okay, enough fantasy. Not that you won't achieve the dreams you have, but before you do, you are going to have to do some things you may never have had to do before. You are going to have to adjust to a lifestyle that may initially be somewhat diminished from your life now, or you are going to find yourself working 24/7. In short, you are going to have to pay your dues!

How Most People Get Started as Consultants

If you weren't recruited right from grad school by one of the big consulting firms, chances are you will come to consulting from the professional route you chose earlier. The idea of becoming a consultant seldom looms large in most people's minds—until they meet and work with a few consultants while doing the work some employer pays them to do. Consulting suddenly appears to be glamorous, and it seems to offer the potential for greater and faster personal growth. This is usually true, but these benefits come at a cost—the most obvious one that of employment stability.

The U.S. Bureau of Labor Statistics in its most recent report on the field has predicted that employment in management, technical, and scientific consulting is expected to grow 76 percent by 2016. This figure was issued prior to the current economic slowdown, but even if it's off drastically in either direction, employment in the consulting field will expand. There is no reliable data on how home-based individual consultancies will fare over the same period, but from everything I have seen, this part of the business should probably expand even more rapidly. The report concludes, "All areas of consulting should experience strong growth."

The BLS concluded: "Management, scientific, and technical consulting services is projected to be one of the fastest growing industries over the next decade. However, because of the number of people looking for work in this industry, competition is expected to be keen." Remember, the BLS is talking about people who are employed as consultants. Consulting is, without question, a growth industry, and there is more than enough room for those who plan to start their own home-based consultancy.

This is a rosy picture, but most roses have some thorns, and I would be remiss if I didn't discuss some of the pitfalls that will result from the current economic downturn. Executive search firms, for example, will more than likely have far more individual than corporate clients. More people will be competing for a diminishing number of openings. However, as corporate staffing is trimmed, more and more companies will have to turn to outside consultants to do the work.

Consulting Is a Growth Industry

U.S. REPORT OPTIMISTIC

This is what the Bureau of Labor Statistics concluded about the future of self-employed consulting:

"The management, scientific, and technical consulting services industry offers excellent opportunities for self-employment. Because capital requirements are low, highly experienced workers can start their own businesses fairly easily and cheaply; indeed, every year, thousands of workers in this industry go into business for themselves. Some of these workers come from established management, scientific, and technical consulting services firms, whereas others leave industry, government, or academic jobs to start their own businesses. Still others remain employed in their primary organizations, but have their own consulting jobs on the side."

The Beginnings

Most of the consultants I know got their start as employees of firms other than consulting practices. Some were engineers; others were in general management, marketing, sales, and human resources. As they climbed the corporate ladder, the range of better positions quite naturally got smaller. And, of course, this meant that the time between promotions got longer. When they saw what consultants did for the firms they worked for, the seed was planted.

Most told of having heart-to-heart talks with their employers, during which the employer offered them extensive consulting work if they were going to leave the firm for better opportunities. One of my friends accepted a job with another firm, moving up from manager of marketing to marketing VP of a competitive firm. His employer couldn't match the offer, but didn't want to lose a good man. So, my friend's soon-to-be ex-employer offered to engage him as a consultant; thus was born a consulting firm with immediate revenue.

This brings up a major issue—money. It is true that running a home-based consultancy is a very cost-effective way to go, but you will still need a steady income stream to at least cover your nut until you are launched and well on the road to success. I talk about this in some detail in chapter 6, but for now, keep in mind that you must plan not only for the day you step off the plank, but for all the days that follow.

A consultant I met a few years ago got her start by being fired. During the last economic downturn in the U.S., she was told that her job was being eliminated. She was given six months' severance and a year of health-care benefits, and sent off with the good wishes of those who stood to benefit from carrying one less salary on their books.

Although she had all the credentials to make it in information technology consulting, she decided that it was time to reorder her priorities and do something that truly appealed to her for the long term. Her part-time passion was writing, and she'd had quite a few articles published every year in the popular and trade press. She discovered that many of the articles in the magazines that had published her material had either been done with extensive collaboration or by ghost writers. All it took was a few calls to the heads of public relations departments of major firms near her before she had more work than she could handle. She could have expanded, but wanted to stay small, work from home, and have full control over the work. So, she gradually raised her fees and now she is very much in demand by corporate clients for all sorts of writing assignments, including speech writing.

There probably are as many ways to get into consulting as there are people already working in the field. Instead of trying to emulate what someone else has done, it's best by far to plan your own path to suit your individual skills and ambitions, and to match the market (or markets) in which you can work. With the Internet being such an entrenched and productive communications tool, you don't even have to think about finding clients in your backyard. I live a few miles from New York City and have clients scattered all over the country. When I was active as a literary agent, I had clients all over the world.

Again, from the most recent Bureau of Labor Statistics report: "Globalization will continue to provide numerous opportunities for consulting firms wishing to expand their services, or help clients expand into foreign markets. The growth of international business will create numerous opportunities for logistics consulting firms as businesses seek to improve coordination in the expanding network of suppliers and consumers."

Meet Ivan Rebolledo

Ivan is the managing partner of TerraNova Partners, an international consulting firm specializing in the Andean region of Latin America. His firm advises clients on economic and political risk, corporate social responsibility, legislative monitoring, strategic corporate communications, and international government relations. He is president of the Bolivian-American Chamber of Commerce, and prior to starting TerraNova, Ivan had a distinguished career with the United Nations in various senior-level executive positions. His clients include many of Latin America's presidents and corporate leaders. And he does all this from a home-based office in New York.

He does, however, make use of a network of worldwide offices that are available at a moment's notice through a commercial service. Ivan says, "Opportunities are available everywhere, and operating from the comfort of a home office with access to offices and facilities all over the world makes it possible for me to focus on my work and not to have to pay attention to the problems of owning real estate and maintaining local staffing." When you think of home-based businesses, the people who run them are as varied and successful as those who own or rent offices away from home.

Putting Yourself in the Picture

Unless you already have some consulting experience, the following exercises can help give you an idea of what you might expect of your life as a consultant. If you count some consultants among your friends, talk with them and share your ideas, dreams, and fears with them. You might even ask if you could accompany one of them on an assignment where you wouldn't be in the way and could just be a passive observer. In the meantime, here are some of the better ways to get a feel for what you might be facing without taking the big plunge.

Think of Yourself as a Consultant

If you are working in the field in which you plan to consult, create a mind-set that helps you see yourself not as an employee, but as a consultant on assignment to your employer. Get a sense of how you would relate to the people in the company as a consultant, not as an employee. Think about what you might do or say differently. Consider the time you currently spend on a project as an employee, and how you might make use of that time if you were a consultant.

The main thing to look for when you do this kind of role-play is the comfort level you have with each activity, relative to how comfortable you are with it now as an employee. Try to envision how you might apportion your time on a project as a consultant as compared to an employee doing the same job. You may be surprised at how much this exercise can change your perspective on your current job. Even if you don't become a consultant, the insight you get will more than likely make you a more productive—and more promotable—employee.

Think Big

Being self-employed is mind-opening. As an employee, you probably think in terms of what works best for each level of supervision above you, tailoring your activities and responses accordingly. As a self-employed, home-based consultant, you have no one to answer to but yourself and your clients. This may surprise you, but just having actual conversations with yourself will open some pretty tightly closed mental doors for you. (Do it where no one else can hear you or your career as a consultant may have to be put on hold to avoid the man with the butterfly net.)

More than just thinking big, do some exercises that give you hard evidence of what it will be like when you go it alone. The best reality test is to run some numbers on what it will cost you to be in business. These will be guesstimates, but they will probably give you numbers close enough to reality for you to start seeing just what you will be facing. Even if the numbers end up being way off, you will have experienced the process of financial planning and management.

While your initial business will be home-based, you may want to think about when and why you might want to expand beyond a home office—say, if your business flourishes. Just keep in mind that bigger is not always better. However, if bigger works for you, be sure to visualize the benefits and the problems of expansion. I have talked with consultants who have gone from solo practice to an out-of-home office with employees; for many of them, the thing that bothers them most is becoming a manager of a business rather than a solver of other people's problems. This may work for you and it may not. As long as you have built a reputation for solid performance and integrity, no one really cares whether you work from a fancy office or from a home office.

Visualize Your Trajectory

This is really an exercise in setting goals and planning to attain them. Starting with specific goals in mind gives you plenty of flexibility to choose the paths you will take and the tools you will use to get where you want to be. Suppose, for example, that one of your goals is based on your idea of what your annual income should be. You could choose to attain that figure by seeking a number of smaller clients whose billing would allow you to reach that figure; or, you could choose to have fewer but better-paying clients to arrive at the same figure. There's some safety in having more clients rather than fewer, but there's usually more work involved with a larger client base. While having fewer clients allows you to focus on fewer problems, if you should lose one of your clients, you could be in financial trouble.

Your trajectory visualization should be process-oriented. That is, you should envision the steps you will take, the order in which you will take them, and the criteria by which you will judge whether or not you have achieved them. It's not as big a deal as you might imagine—unless you want to get down to the nitpicky details. At this point in your planning, I strongly suggest that you avoid the minutiae and just try to focus on the major elements and how you can put them together.

Without getting into a finely tuned plan and outline, it's usually a good idea to summarize the major elements of your business trajectory on paper. Apart from how you will use this plan later, it's nice to have something concrete to show for your effort; that's what the gold stars are for in kindergarten. (They work just as well for highly educated adults!)

Visualize Your Work Day as a Consultant

Since you have probably never been a consultant, this might be a little difficult. However, your current work experience will probably serve as a good model for this exercise. No matter what kind of work you are currently doing, you have had related experiences that you can draw on as you consider the primary work of a consultant.

For example, suppose you're a sales manager for the firm that currently employs you, and the marketing director has asked you to determine how your sales force will implement a recently announced marketing plan. Everything you would do for the marketing director as a sales manager you would do for him as a consultant. The major difference would be in the relationship you have with the person who gives you the assignment, and the fact that as a consultant, you would probably not be responsible for implementing the ideas.

Most of the personal issues you have as an employee would probably not be present in your role as a consultant. However, you will experience a different set of events when you consult. You are usually hired to solve a problem that someone inside the company has failed to solve. If you have to interact with the person whose plan was rejected, you will not be an especially welcome guest. It's a different story if you've been engaged to create plans for new projects. Although resentment can be present in many consulting situations, most can be easily defused simply by allowing the resentful party to share in the work—and the glory.

This visualization exercise is sort of an internalized role-playing situation. If you use it to think beyond the edges of your current experience, you will see what I mean. Remember: While it's important to recognize the downside of consulting, you should also look at the bright side as well.

Visualize Yourself as You Relate to Others

It's a mistake to think that your business relationships will be the same when you're a consultant as they are when you're an employee. I know quite a few consultants who continue to consult for companies that formerly employed them. Many of them claim that some relationships got stronger while others deteriorated; it all depends on the individuals involved. You should be prepared for the shifts.

As far as new clients are concerned, try to see yourself as someone who has been hired to do something that could not be done inside. This could be because the company doesn't have the in-house talent to do the work, or it could be because those who tried to solve the problem were unable to do so. You will be seen as a hero by some, and in less flattering terms by others.

The main goal of this exercise is for you to see just how comfortable (or uncomfortable) you will be in the role of a consultant. In general, you will probably discover that your comfort levels with most people will be about the same, except that the individuals you deal with will react differently to you than they do now as an employee. You should be prepared to play new and different roles as a consultant—a small price to pay for the benefit of being on your own.

Be Aware That Failure May Be an Option in Some Cases

There are two clichés that motivational speakers and writers love to throw around. One is that failure is not an option. When was the last time you met someone who has not failed at something? The other is that you should learn from every experience. You will always learn more from your goofs than you will from those things that earn applause. So, failure is always possible, and you will learn much more from these disappointments than you will from your successes. Maintaining this attitude is especially important for a consultant.

How do you respond to criticism now? Are you especially hard on yourself when you make a mistake? If you let criticism and mistakes take a big toll on your attitude and behavior as an employee, you just might have difficulty succeeding as a consultant. If you assume that you will make an occasional mistake and are willing to face up to it with your boss or your client, you will not only have a more comfortable life, but you will also send a message to your clients that you know you are not perfect. However (and this is very important), you must also send the message that you are aware of your mistake and accept whatever blame may be handed out—and that you will do everything you can to correct the problem.

This brings up an issue that has sunk more than a few consultants very early in their careers: They oversell the clients on what they can do. It's a common tendency in all of us. We want to appear more competent than our competitors. Unless you are absolutely, positively certain that you will succeed, it's best to present yourself as someone who will do their level best, while acknowledging that you are not perfect. You don't have to admit that failure is an option, but you do have to let the client know that you will do everything you possibly can to solve his or her problem.

How Hard Are You Willing to Work?

Surprisingly, you may find that it's harder to work as someone's employee than it is to be an independent consultant. The real issue, however, is not how hard you work, but how smart you work. Hard work may be pulling an overnighter on a rush report for either your current boss or one of the clients you will soon have. Smart work is making sure the report is completed during the normal work day.

You will often be asked to put in time that you had planned to spend doing something else—and you just can't refuse. Chances are that you will work a lot harder in the first few years of running your own business than you will once it gets established. Learning can be hard work, and learning what works and what doesn't in your new role will take time. Don't spend a lot of time trying to bend situations to fit what you were comfortable with before you became a consultant. Try to be as flexible as you can without allowing others to take unfair advantage of you. It's not easy to say no to a client when you're first starting out, but you'd be surprised at how easy it becomes once you are off and running. It's called learning the ropes.

Part of that initial hard work will be put toward establishing a client base. Most beginning consultants get one-shot assignments more than long-term engagements. This means that you will be spending a lot of time looking for work. Once you prove yourself, you will get more assignments from clients who are happy with your work, and you can cut back on your prospecting. However, never get so complacent that you stop looking for new clients altogether. If your prospecting brings you more work than you can handle, take it on and share the load with trusted associates. Few client relationships last forever, especially when your specialty is not process work, but specific problem solving. New business development should be an ongoing activity, no matter how busy you are. I discuss this in detail in chapter 10.

The Financial Factors

Few people who go into consulting have a clear idea of what is involved on the financial side. This is the subject of chapters 6 and 7, but for now, here are some items and issues to think about:

- Will you start your business with money you already have, or will you have to borrow to get things rolling?
- If you do borrow money, where will you get it?
- Can you survive for at least a year with absolutely no income from the business?
- If you need capital, would you consider taking on a partner to supply the money?
- What is the bare minimum you need to live on if your business is taking off, but is taking longer than you anticipated?

You may be planning to work from your home office just to start (or even forever), but it's a mistake to think that simply because you are working from home you will have no office expenses. You may not pay yourself rent initially, but your home operating expenses—such as heating, electricity, water, and waste disposal—should be factored into your budget planning.

Borrowed money is often the basis of home-based consulting businesses, but its source can often cause serious problems later on. Borrow from family members and they probably won't hound you for payments the same way a bank might—but family members remember and can hold grudges of mountainous proportions if you fail to pay on time.

Too many consulting practices get started with a partner or two, mainly to ensure adequate capitalization. Whether you take on full-time or silent partners primarily for their money, they can become a problem. I'll fill you in on this issue in chapters to come, but for now, I just want you to be aware that you might get more than money and a silent partner when you go this route.

When you create your business plan, you will have to include a serious look at what it will take to survive until the business can support itself, let alone make a profit. Too many nascent consultants bite the dust because they refuse to adjust their mode of living in the early stages of the business. Quite apart from the financial considerations, you will have to look at your own lifestyle. It's not easy to go from two cars to one—especially if more than one family member will be using it. It's not easy to cancel vacations, or to skip concerts, trips to the theater, and other family outings, especially if you and your spouse have a growing family. Think about it: Is your family willing to put up with a little (or even a lot) less during the time you think it will take to get your home-based consulting business off the ground?

Filling in the Blanks in Your Experience Base

Suppose you are a marketing person and know your field cold. Is that all you need to make it? Far from it! You need to know how to plan and run a business, as well as how to help solve your clients' marketing problems. You may have to take a course or two on small-business accounting. And, if you're smart, you will continue to learn what's new in the field in which you consult. This may mean taking courses offered by associations you might belong to, enrolling in continuing education programs at a local school or college, or even taking some of the currently popular distance-learning courses.

All of this means a financial obligation, as well as a commitment of time and energy. In most states certain professionals (i.e., doctors, dentists, and other health-care workers) are required to take courses in order to renew their state-issued licenses. It will probably never be required of management consultants, but you'll know you need to increase your "learning" when your clients start turning to your competitors.

Many fields that include consultants in their rolls offer continuing education programs and member certification. The Public Relations Society of America (www .prsa.org), for example, has extensive programs scheduled every year for members who want to upgrade their skills. If this is your field, you'd be wise to check out what is available from this very progressive organization.

1. *Is it a wise move to start a consulting business on the side while employed full-time by another company?*

    It probably isn't, especially if you happen to be presently employed by a consulting firm. Needless to say, anyone is free to do whatever he or she wants during their off hours, unless you have a contract that specifically restricts you from certain activities. It's not unusual for people to take off-hour freelance projects from time to time, mainly to supplement their current income. But, if you are really serious about becoming a full-time consultant, get started on the right foot and make the move when it's convenient. This doesn't mean that you shouldn't try to line up clients for when you will be consulting full-time. In fact, you should do everything you can to ensure that you have work in hand before you open your doors.

2. *Are there cycles in the consulting business that make opening your doors at one time better than another?*

    There are, but they relate only to the fields in which you plan to specialize. You should know these cycles well if you are presently employed in your field. In general, however, it's probably better to be in business for a few months before consulting budgets are set in your field.

03 When Your Home Is More than Just Where You Live

Never apologize for working from a home office!

Early in my solo career I had a consulting assignment from a major book publisher which required fairly regular contact with the CEO. I had only been in business a few years, worked from a home office, and was not considered one of the heavies in the field. During one of my late-morning sessions with the CEO, he suggested that we go to lunch.

There I was, a newbie, probably going to be stuck for a big lunch and trying to hold my own with the head of a major book publishing company. To my surprise, he said, "You know, Bert, I really envy you." I didn't know whether this was a touch of sarcasm or what. But it turned out that this man, who had worked up to his present job as head of a world-class publishing company, was thinking of calling it quits and starting a one-man publishing consulting business. He wasn't under fire from the stockholders, and his performance record was the envy of most honchos at publishing companies his size and larger. He just liked the idea of working from home! Sadly, he never realized his dream. Shortly after our lunch he was diagnosed with an illness that took him very quickly.

It was that lunch experience that put it all in perspective for me. People were actually envious of my working from a home office. None that I knew of ever saw me as any less effective because I worked from home. I was getting plenty of assignments, and my business was growing.

At one point I considered hiring someone and renting office space, but Louie, my accountant, gave me the advice I needed to keep me from making that mistake. I had asked him to run the numbers for me, to tell me what an employee, an office space, and the associated expenses might be. He told me that I could afford it, but then asked me why I wanted to do it.

Although I hadn't really thought about building a bigger business, my current successes seemed to indicate that I should grow, that I should move out of my home office. Louie pointed out that he had big clients and still worked from a small home office that backed up on a view of a beautiful reservoir. He had decided years ago that big was not for him. He had small pieces of business from major corporations that paid their bills on time, and the water company that owned the reservoir had given him a key to a gate near his home so he could come and go with a fishing pole anytime he wanted.

I was hooked. Louie and I caught a mess of perch and bluegills that day, fried them for dinner on his veranda, and I have never thought again about doing anything but working from my home office.

You may be different. You may see a home office as just a launching pad to bigger and better things. That's fine—but before you make any major commitments, find your "Louie" and have a heart-to-heart, not just about the money it would cost and what you could make, but about lifestyle issues.

There are as many benefits and drawbacks to working solo from your home as there are to moving out and moving up. Make sure it's what you want from life that wins out. Don't let the fad of the day push you into something you may someday regret. You've ironed out most of the wrinkles in working from a home office. Moving into an office space could turn out to be an old concept in a new and dazzling costume. My guess is that in the near future you will be seeing a lot of office space becoming available at very attractive prices. Think it through before you jump at any of these bargains. It may be the best thing that could happen to you—or it may be the worst.

Even if you do decide to grow, you can expand without having anything but a home office. More than a few of the larger consulting operations are set up for each employee or partner to work from his or her home office. With the convenience of fax machines, the Internet, and cell phones, a fancy office just isn't necessary. One of my neighbors here in New Jersey works for a consulting company on the West Coast. Once or twice a year he schleps out there for a collective chin-wag, but other than that, all business is done by phone, fax, and Internet.

What About the Office Itself?

As you may have gathered, I have been in quite a few home offices. Every one is different. Some are purely utilitarian, while others are elegant. Some are huge and others quite small. In fact, I once met a consultant who worked from a closet, and it wasn't even a walk-in closet. It was an ordinary-size clothes closet located in a spare bedroom in his house.

You had to see this setup to believe it. He had designed a roll-out office that filled the entire closet, with about two inches' clearance on each side of the door. Everything fit in flush with the back wall of the closet. It was fully wired for lights, phones, and power cords and cables that uncoiled as he rolled out his office, and re-coiled when he slid it in at the end of the day. His desk surface was a pullout, and he had file drawers, a kneehole, and his office equipment built right in. I was in Submarine Six when I was in the navy, and I have to say that this marvel of functional design would have been the envy of the designer of the Gato-Class boats in the squadron. When he rolled it back and closed the door there was no evidence at all of an office, and he had full use of the bedroom for guests. He just gave up a closet, but that was a small price to pay.

To Hide It or Let It All Hang Out

If you have plenty of space, especially a room that can be dedicated to office use, it's probably best to make it a one-use setup rather than trying to disguise it with some multiuse furniture. This way, you can leave files and papers scattered around, and unfinished tasks don't have to be packed and stored at the end of the day.

A home office should be thought of as more than just a place to work. Sticking to the notion that form follows function may be tempting, but since you will probably spend a lot of time in your home office, I'd suggest that you plan as carefully for its comfort factors as you do for its practicality.

Where in the house should the home office be? First and foremost, it should be out of the way of everybody and everything else. After that, you are left with aesthetic and functional issues to solve. If you prefer a space with few distractions, choose a spot with few windows, where you are less likely to be interrupted by family members. If a view of the outside world is to your liking, your choice is obvious.

I preferred a view of my yard, and thus located my first home office in a second-floor room overlooking the garden, trees, and plantings. Now, we have the fourth-floor penthouse of a 1908 stone school that was converted to home condominiums. I look down on treetops and church steeples, and in the distance I can see the ridge of the Palisades. Distracting? Of course—but there's more to work than just cranking out books, reports, and client projects.

Very early in my career I was represented by a literary agent of considerable repute in the publishing field. Prior to his escape from the corporate world, he had cofounded a major publishing company and edited some of the authors you may have read. His home in Connecticut was in the woods, just where he liked it. His office was simply his dining-room table. In the morning he got out the files he wanted to work on and went to work. This was pre-computer, so all he had was a landline telephone that he put on the table in the morning and put away when work was over. It worked for him then and could work for you today. Just keep it simple and any place will work.

What About the Outside?

The legal issues of the exterior appearance of your office are discussed in detail in chapter 9, but you should be aware of some of the problems you will face in the context of this chapter. If your consulting work will involve people coming and going to your home office, you may come face-to-face with some cranky neighbors, and even the local tax assessor. Every state, county, town, borough, and burg has its own laws governing business use of residential property.

Some towns insist that there be a separate exterior door leading directly to your home office, especially if there will be a lot of traffic. Some will insist that you adhere to local parking ordinances that were designed to keep cars from clogging downtown shopping parking spots, not residential areas. Some town ordinances strictly prohibit anyone from running a home office in certain residential zones. Consultants who live and work in these tightly restricted areas, with little or no client traffic, simply keep their work to themselves. They will tell you that as long as the

> **Home Office Tip . . .**
>
> To avoid annoying the neighbors when you might have to have several clients visit you, consider making arrangements with a local restaurant for a quiet location. If you don't have visitors often, the occasional cost of a lunch meeting is worth it to keep peace with neighbors. A consultant I heard of recently is a member of the local chapter of a large national service club. The chapter in his town has its own building and allows members to use some of the rooms for business meetings if they book far enough in advance.

neighbors are not bothered by strangers coming and going and cars being parked in front of their property, most people don't care that you work at home.

If this is your situation, you may still want to keep it to yourself. Even if you never have a client visit you, you may have a neighbor who, for whatever reason, wants to turn you in. Your neighbors may think you are unemployed when you don't catch the 7:15 train every morning with the rest of them, but being a person of mystery can leave a lot of room for either envy or endless neighborhood speculation. Play it for all it's worth, but play your cards close to your vest when it comes to anything that could lead the sheriff to your door with a notice of residential noncompliance!

If you will be having clients visit you, do whatever is needed to comply with your local ordinances and the anticipated whims of your "friendly" neighbors. Err on the side of the law; don't take chances. If you just can't wait, turn to chapter 9 and you will see why some accountants think it's better to not even declare that you have a home office, even though you might be able to deduct a portion of your utilities on your taxes. Otherwise, let's move along.

What's Needed in Every Good Consultant's Home Office

Since I don't know whether you are thinking about engineering or management consulting, or some other field, I have limited this section to the basics. You engineers may need specialized CAD programs and hardware. Management and financial consultants will need communications equipment that others may not see as being valuable to them. But everyone has to communicate, so let's go there first.

Telephone Service

Before we get into the details, let me warn you that relying on your residential line for all your communications is a prescription for disaster. Being in the middle of a client call on a residential line when your teenager picks up the extension and says, "How much longer are you going to be, Dad?" is not going to do much to enhance your professional status. More than that, unless you have a special reason for doing it, never give out your personal home phone number. Just make sure that clients who might have emergency situations have a way of getting in touch with you. Cell phones are best used in this case. Pagers seem to be history now.

Business lines can be more expensive than residential lines, but unless you want your business listed in the Yellow Pages, you may not have to go the business-line route. These rules vary with different phone companies all over the country, and you will have to check this out for yourself. If you choose a residential line for your business, the business name will appear only in the White Pages. This may be all you need.

Even the least expensive telephones have built-in answering facilities now, so separate answering machines (and even answering services) will probably not be necessary. Check your local phone company to see if the line you choose has a call-forwarding service. With this you can have calls made to your home office line directed to another site, such as your cell phone. This way you will get your office calls when you are out of the office, without having to wait until you return to collect all the messages that have piled up. The technology changes so rapidly that what I am describing may be greatly improved and enhanced by the time you read this book. It's important to carefully consider what each carrier has to offer.

Home Office Tip . . .

It may be different by the time you read this, but as of now, you can't attach your fax to a cell phone. If your business requires heavy use of a fax, you will probably have to have a wired landline.

Fax and Copy Machines

You will probably need a copier and a fax machine, but before you spring for separate units, check out the computer printers that also include copying and faxing functions. You will probably pay less for a multiuse machine than for separate units. However, if any one of the features quits on you and you have to have the machine repaired, you will be without the other services you probably need to keep your office running. My advice would be to get one machine that does faxing and copying, and one that serves as a printer. You will probably have more need for the printer than you will the other machines, and the cost of printers is low enough these days that you're not looking at a big expense. I was shocked the other day to see that the cost of a replacement cartridge for my plain vanilla laser printer came close to what it would cost to buy a new printer. The hook here, of course, is that the new machine comes with a very limited-use cartridge, and long before the machine bites the dust you will have to spring for the expensive cartridge replacement anyway.

Here are a few things to keep in mind when considering a copier:

- Estimate how many copies you are likely to make in an average month.
- Will you need to collate and staple any of your copies?
- Will you want to copy both sides of any of your work?
- Will you need high-enough resolution to copy art and photos?
- Is color copying an issue?
- Will you have to copy letter-size as well as legal-size documents?
- Will most of your copies be text or images? If you can avoid getting a machine that has all the bells and whistles, you will save a lot on the initial cost as well as the cartridge replacement costs. A simple but high-quality laser printer is usually more than adequate for most consulting needs.

Most copiers are pretty durable, but it can cost more to fix one that doesn't work and is out of warranty than it does to buy a new one. The insurance policies the dealers want to sell you are seldom really worth it. If one of these machines is going to quit because of faulty parts or manufacturing, it will probably do so within the standard warranty period.

Fax machines, or the fax features of a combination machine, will probably include more than you really need unless you plan to send a lot of photos, drawings, and documents that include handwriting.

Here are some things to consider before purchasing a fax machine:

- How often will you need to send or receive a document that is only available now as a printed piece of paper? If your printer has scanner capability, chances are that your office computer program includes a subroutine for faxing whatever you can store digitally. You should also be able to receive similar documents and be able to print them on your standard computer printer.
- Will you need capability to send both letter- and legal-size documents?
- Will a stand-alone fax take up space that you could put to better use with something else?

A few years ago, faxing was the big thing. It's still a practical way to send certain types of documents. However, if you can get away with a printer that has a scanner and use the fax program that came with your computer's office program, I'd suggest that you go this route. I avoid faxing anything except legal documents and documents with drawings, pictures, or handwriting that must be reproduced on the other end. I refuse to do any editorial work with fax. It's so much easier and more productive to do it all right on-screen with any of the widely used word processing programs.

As your consulting business grows, you will probably have to adjust your thinking about fax machines, copiers, and printers. Each of these devices is a lot less expensive than they were just a few short years ago. Play it by ear, but consider everything when you see one system being overused and another gathering dust.

The One Machine You Can't Do Without

No, it's not the coffeemaker—it's the computer! But you already knew that, didn't you? As far as I can see, you will not survive without a computer—it's as plain as that. The real question becomes, Will you work with an office PC and a separate laptop for work in the field, or should you consider buying one of the heavy-duty laptops that can serve you well both in the office and in the field?

It's really tempting to go the beefed-up portable route, but I would advise against it. Having two machines means that you can back up all your stuff so it's present on both machines. A relatively inexpensive PC and similar laptop will probably cost about the same, or possibly a little more than one good heavy-duty portable machine. Having two means that you will always be able to work while one is being fixed. It also means that your data can be backed up quickly and available immediately on both machines.

A crash on one machine means that the original software package must be reinstalled in the repaired machine and that all the backed-up data must be installed. Most backup programs handle only data, not programs you may have installed yourself. By keeping two machines in complete sync, you are ready to go without all the fuss when one bites the dust. This is what I do. I have an older laptop that is pretty much a mirror image of what I have on a stand-alone office PC. I don't live with the same fear of the dreaded blue screen as most of my friends do. By the way, if you don't want to invest in a new backup laptop, pick up a used machine, have a pro go over it and bring it up to speed, and you will pay about half of what you would have to pay for a new portable. I bought my backup laptop new about eight years ago, and while it has few of the current bells and whistles, it's perfect for all of my text operations.

You can choose from a huge number of machines and almost as many different computer manufacturers. This is not a paid plug, but over the years I have had nine computers, and all from Dell. I've never had a serious problem, and they quickly resolved the few minor problems I did have. I'm sure that many of the other manufacturers are at least as good, or maybe even better, than Dell. But, for what's it's worth, give them a shot with the others you might consider.

Buy New or Upgrade?

The answer to this question depends almost entirely on your old computer and whether or not it is capable of doing what you need it to do. Just because a computer

Home Office Tip . . .

Don't throw away or give away your old computer when you upgrade to a new one. As long as it is working and will handle the software you plan to use on a new machine, keep the clunker as a backup. If it's slow, chances are that it's because you have pretty much crammed your hard drive with stuff you either never used or used only occasionally. Think about reformatting the hard drive on your old machine to get rid of all the clutter and installing only the programs you use for your business. Keep your Internet connection software, of course; once you've cleaned the junk off your hard drive, you'll be surprised at how fast it will run.

is old is not a good reason to abandon it. I've been told that most computers and other electronic office equipment will fail early on if they are going to fail at all. And in most cases your warranty will probably cover the cost of repair or replacement. Once a machine has had its shakedown cruise, it will probably last longer than you want it to. That is, it will keep on working when you really want to upgrade to the new super XXX machine that does a lot more than your hardworking old machine.

As long as your computer is working well, is fast enough to do what you want it to do, and has the storage capability you need, stick with it. The things that usually call for upgrade can be handled with investing in another printer. If your computer is capable of handling upgraded software such as a new operating system or any of the programs you use routinely, you should be okay. And when you run out of memory, you can either install new memory boards in the machine, or you can pick up a new external hard drive for around a hundred bucks that can possibly give you even more storage capacity than you have in the onboard memory. So, it boils down to speed, memory, and the ability to run newer software efficiently.

Having said this, however, you should always keep your eye out for bargains. When you are forced to buy a new machine because your old one died, you are at the mercy of the current pricing. When new models are being introduced, and after holidays when computers are often given as gifts, you can usually pick up some very good bargains.

Peripherals and Software

Most computers today are pretty much self-contained. That is, they have built-in modems, multiple USB ports, and Ethernet connections. The software that accompanies most new computers is usually just right for a start-up consulting business. You will probably be given the choice of a home or professional version of Word. The professional version is quite a bit more expensive than the home version, but it has been my experience that the home edition has everything I need to run my business from home. You may need more bells and whistles, but it is a good idea to check it out rather than assume that the plain vanilla version of Word won't suit your needs.

If you plan to use some heavy-duty programs for graphics, such as one of the CAD programs, make sure it will run on your machine. If you have a new machine that has only USB ports, but you have some older peripheral hardware that requires an RS232 port, there are simple in-line adapters you can buy for under $20 that will allow you to use older externally connected hardware.

Simply because your computer may have a bunch of USB ports, don't hook up everything you own to them. The more software-driven peripherals you have attached, the slower your machine will run. Remember: One of the big advantages of USB ports is that they allow you to add and remove hardware without having to shut down, connect, and reboot as was necessary with the older serial ports. Keep your machine lean and mean!

Most computers are sold today with flat-screen displays. I still see some machines offered with CRT displays, however. Just remember that the flat screen display takes up a lot less space and it uses considerably less power than does a CRT display.

The Internet
It's safe to say that you probably won't be able to do business unless you have an Internet connection and can use it efficiently and effectively. There's plenty of help available on the subject from books, friends, or courses at local continuing education programs.

Most Internet connections today are made through high-speed connections to your telephone line and through the company that provides your telephone service. You can also access the Net through cable and satellite connections. You can even still get on via a slow dial-up connection, but this is definitely not the way to go. Armed with a Wi-Fi-enabled laptop, you should be able to access the Internet without needing to make any wired connection from just about every location in the country.

I return to computers later in chapters 10 and 11 when I discuss marketing your services. The Internet is not only the fastest way to communicate, but it's also becoming one of the better ways to acquire business for both new and established consulting businesses.

Stationery, Business Cards, Letterhead, and Other Printed Material

Even though most of your communicating will probably be done by way of the Internet and telephone, the need for stationery and business cards still exists. With the right software and printer, you can not only design and print everything you will need, but you can do it on demand rather than having to buy and store boxes of letterhead and envelopes. You can also create your own business cards, but this sometimes requires a small, specialized printer that will handle the small sheets and the card stock.

If this is more than you want to tackle, most local printers have design services available to help you with the creative side, which is what usually causes problems for most new consultants. Here are a few tips to keep you from looking like a total amateur:

- Keep the logo, if you use one, simple. Professional designers will tell you all about the importance of simplicity and functionality.
- Don't try to tell a long story on your card or letterhead.
- Stay away from using a lot of color.
- Choose a simple, uncomplicated, and easy-to-read typeface.
- Look at the letterheads of some of the major consulting firms in your field and you will quickly see that glitz is not the way to go.

Avoid the urge to "stand out" by doing something "different" with your company graphics. Your graphics should resemble those of the established firms in your field without actually copying them.

Frequently Asked Questions

1. *Is it practical to have part-time secretarial help working directly in my office?*
   If you are not anxious to let people know about your home office, someone showing up regularly, even if it's only for a few hours a day, just might tip your hand. You are probably better off finding a part-time office worker who will pack up work, do it at his or her own location, and deliver it when done. As long as this is done on a random basis, your neighbors will probably not notice the routine and start asking questions.

2. *What about those shared offices that are available in some areas?*
   If they are well run and staffed, they can be an excellent adjunct to a home office. Many of these services have conference room space that, when booked in advance, can be used for client meetings. The services I've seen

have been well appointed and provide excellent office work backup. You can use some of these on a part-time basis, or you might even consider using one in place of a home office. Check them out!

3. *My home office is not in a house, but in my condominium. The bylaws only talk about office and professional signage, mainly because there are doctors' offices on the lower floors. Although no one has complained, should I let the association know that I work from my home office?*

If there are no specific prohibitions stated in your condominium agreement, just leave it alone; continue to be a good unit owner and neighbor.

04 Your Business Plan Is Your Road Map

Not everyone who starts a consulting business writes a business plan. I don't have facts to back this up, but I would guess that most of those who succeed did write a plan, and those who didn't write one either had a much harder time of it, or they didn't make it at all.

I didn't write a business plan when I started my business thirty-eight years ago. I was well educated, had solid experience in my field, and thought, Why waste time? I won't bore you with the details, but it was a big mistake. *A business plan is not a waste of time.* Apart from providing you with some working guidelines once you get going, a plan also forces you to focus as you have never focused before—and believe me, this is a critical factor in starting a business.

You have dreamed about having your own business, you have read the success stories, and you may have even met people who have lived the dream. It's exciting. It's a new beginning. It's also a trap for those who don't plan for every eventuality.

A business plan is especially important for consultants because there are usually no products involved. If you need a loan to get started, the first thing a lender is likely to ask is what you have as collateral. Your good reputation doesn't count for very much. The banker can't turn that into cash any more than you could if you don't make it. But, I'm getting ahead of the story. What follows is a step-by-step approach to writing a business plan specifically for a consulting business, and especially a consulting business that will operate from a home office.

In broad strokes, your business plan will define your business, list your goals, and describe what you bring to the table. If done properly, it will help you to allocate the resources you already have and provide a plan for the acquisition of the resources that you must acquire. It should be able to help you predict where and what the rough spots might be, and how you should go about overcoming them. And it should point the way to systems you can use to manage progress.

A carefully conceived business plan should have milestones to help you determine whether or not you are on the right track. And probably most important, a good business plan should provide alternatives for course corrections as you sail along. No matter how carefully you plan, it will always be necessary to make changes. Some of those changes will involve major shifts in direction, while others will involve ways to ratchet up the things you are doing right. Your plan should not be a straitjacket, but it should be rigid enough to keep you on track and flexible enough to allow you to drop things that aren't working and switch to better alternatives.

Begin by Defining Your Company

Do you really have to define the company you plan to start? After all, what is more obvious than the fact that a consulting company is going to provide consulting services—right? Well, not quite. For example, will you provide only analysis and solutions to a client's problems, or will you also take an active part in the implementation of the solutions you offer? Typically, there are no products involved in consulting, but there could be if, for example, your solution to a client's problem includes specially written software. Will you produce these products, or will you work with someone else to back you up?

Your definition should include a list of the business's major strengths relative to the services you plan to offer. It should also identify where you have weaknesses, especially where you might be unable to offer the complete package called for by a client's assignment. If you plan to addresses these weaknesses internally, describe how that will be done. Will you hire people, or make strategic alliances with others who can provide what you can't?

You should clearly define your personal objectives and the goals you have for your company. Get specific here. Where do you expect to be in a year? Five years? Do you plan to remain small, or are you planning to build a larger organization? What do you see for yourself in terms of personal self-improvement that might be required to start and build the business? This could include formal schooling, distance learning, or simply identifying your weak areas so that you can strengthen them by your day-to-day work experiences.

Which form of ownership will be most practical for the business you envision? There are real advantages and disadvantages to each. The choice most often boils down to whether you will form a traditional corporation or a limited liability corporation. You will find that for almost every positive factor in one form, there's a corresponding negative factor. For example, go one way and you will be allowed some tax-carry-forward opportunities. Go another and you will discover that you must close your books at the end of every year and not benefit from this carry-forward feature. I discuss this in greater detail in chapter 8, but I just want you to be aware for now that "what you make on the tomatoes you will lose on the potatoes," to use an old saying. However, the decision you make will be a lot easier when you have clearly defined the company you are planning to start.

And, of course, you should have a pretty clear picture of who your clients will be. Will you be aiming at major corporations, or will your clients be smaller? Who will you focus on first within your target companies to get the assignments you need, and who will you actually work with once you get assignments? You should also have a general description of how you plan to bring in the business.

The Services You Plan to Offer

Most solo consultants tend to focus on narrow areas, especially areas where their larger competitors might be weak. However, you should be aware of why the larger firms are weak in these areas. It might be that the larger firms see there isn't the kind of money they need to survive in a particular service, or it could be that you have a talent which is only needed occasionally by larger consultants, and they don't see it as profitable enough to provide.

This means that you may actually get some assignments from larger consultants as well as from your target market clients. I have met more than a few consultants over the years who do nothing but subcontract consulting for larger consultancies in areas where larger firms are weak and have no need or plans to staff up. More than a few good freelance business writers make more money subcontracting for larger consultancies than they do from the clients for whom they work directly.

If you plan to do subcontract work for larger consultancies, it's important to have a good picture of who they are, where they are located, who their clients are, and the kind of subcontract work you might be likely to get from them. You should also try to determine whether, as a subcontractor, you would be identified by the consultant to the client. It can get sticky when you pitch a client and discover that a consultant for whom you already work is already using you to work on this client's projects.

This is also the point where you should include a detailed plan of your fees and charges. Will you charge by the hour . . . the day . . . the week? Will you charge by the project, or will you provide client services on a retainer basis? (I discuss this further in chapter 6, but you should start giving it some thought now.)

Are there any products related to your service involved? Some consultants, especially those doing training, will provide training materials—books, discs, etc.—that they will buy from publishers. Will you mark up these products, provide them at your cost, or include their cost in the total negotiated fee?

The goal of this section of your business plan is really to make you think beyond the basics. You will probably discover that there are more opportunities available than you thought of originally. And, unless I miss my guess, five years from now your repertoire will include a lot more services than you originally envisioned.

Your Marketing Plan

Your marketing plan is really your work plan. Just about everything else in your business plan will be pretty straightforward, but the need for a comprehensive marketing plan is critical. It's been said that more than a few people who started consulting businesses which proposed to provide marketing services to clients failed simply because the founders didn't have marketing plans for their own businesses. You may be the acknowledged expert in your field, but unless you market your abilities correctly, you will have serious problems. Don't take anything for granted. Nail down all the details!

The best way to begin on the marketing section of your business plan is to dig into all the published information you can lay your hands on. Look in the magazines and journals that cover your field. If your field gets much coverage in general circulation newspapers, use them, too. Check out all the information that is available from federal, state, and local governments, along with trade and professional associations you may belong to, as all of this can be helpful. Make sure that you get current as well as historical data. If you rely only on current information, you will not be able to see the historical trends that could impact your business down the road.

Once you have exhausted all the sources of this secondary data, it will be time to do some primary research on the factors that will have immediate and local impact on what you plan to do. Will there be enough potential clients in your immediate area to make the venture worthwhile? If your business will not depend on local clients, you will have to factor travel expenses into your planning. In other words, after you first determine the health of your target market, you will need to get up close and personal. Now, here are the key issues you need to consider:

Potential Clients

You may already have a general idea of your potential local client base. But to be most helpful, you should try to determine more than just who they might be. You should also try to determine things like how often they will require the services you plan to offer. If your service is one that is used frequently, and there is a significant potential client base in your area, you will probably plan to stay close to home and have minimal travel expenses. If your service is used only occasionally and there might not be a large-enough client base in your immediate area, you will have to plan accordingly.

Once you have a picture of your potential client base, you will be in a good position to determine what it will cost you to develop clients and to service them regularly. I discuss this later, but now is the time to start gathering the information you need to make sound decisions.

Having a clear picture of your potential clients will help you significantly when it comes time to think about how you will price your services. Smaller clients who are not accustomed to working with consultants are often the ones most in need of help, but just as often are either unable to pay for consulting services, or are unable to see the benefit of buying professional advice. Larger companies that have experience working with consultants seldom have to be sold on the idea of seeking outside help and advice. But this is where you will begin to encounter competition from consultants who are already well established in the field. And this, quite naturally, leads to the next item in the marketing portion of your business plan—competition.

Your Competitors

Depending on your field, you will have both direct and indirect competition for your services. Your direct competitors will be those who do exactly what you plan to do. Your indirect competitors will be found within the service companies that your potential clients already work with. If, for example, a potential client works with one of the big accounting firms, that firm may offer the same consulting services that you plan to offer. The accounting firm is in a good position to know when a client needs the help of a consultant, and will have a jump on the business that you would like to acquire. Try to discover what the larger consulting firms offer and what the less-obvious sources of consulting services might be able to provide clients.

As I have said before, smaller firms usually look for niche openings to get their foot in the door. Therefore, you really have to know a lot more about your potential competitors than simply their location and the names of the clients they serve. You really need to know a lot about their individual strengths and weaknesses—especially their weaknesses. And you should also have a clear picture of just how important these weaknesses are to the clients they serve.

If you see yourself building your business by subcontracting a niche service to larger consulting firms, you certainly won't want to offend them by trying to market your services directly to their clients. If, on the other hand, you can determine that the larger consulting firm wouldn't miss the business you could take away from them, then it's open season for you. I get into this in detail in chapter 10, but for now, it's time to collect all the information you can on your competitors.

One of the biggest mistakes beginning consultants make is to take on projects that they are not fully equipped to handle. It's tempting when you've just opened your doors and you need some immediate cash flow—but don't do it!

Use this checklist to identify and qualify your potential competitors:

- The size and qualifications of the staff
- The gross annual billing, as well as the billing in the areas in which you plan to consult
- The reputation of the firm and the reputations of the individual consultants who provide the services you plan to offer
- How difficult it will be to compete with each competitor

As you analyze your competitors, try to envision how you stack up against each one. To help you get a realistic picture, try to envision just how a potential client would evaluate you and your competitor relative to a specific project. Simple checklists can be very helpful here, using the key points a client would consider to be positives and negatives. What you should end up with after this exercise is a rank-order listing of the firms with whom you will compete and a list of your strengths and weaknesses relative to those of your competitors.

Your Single Most Important Strength

In launching any business, whether it's a consulting firm or a candy store, it's critical to get a strong start, mainly to bring in immediate money. Once you get going you can begin the fine-tuning that will ultimately lead you to the business that will work best for you. But for now, just write a very brief statement of what you see as your major strength and how you will use it to launch your business. Don't get windy and loquacious. Be brief, clear, and to the point.

Your Business Development Plans

You can't just hang out a sign and wait for customers to find you. What will you do to get business? The typical consultant often starts out with a client in hand, usually his or her previous employer, and builds from there. However, if you are hitting the trail cold, you will probably find that promotion, publicity, and a public relations approach will be more cost-effective (and work more quickly) than advertising. This is the subject of chapter 10.

Your business plan is a financial tool as well as a working plan, so this is the point where you should insert some numbers—typically, what you have available to spend and what you plan to spend to promote your business. If marketing and sales promotion is not the field in which you plan to consult, I'd suggest that you get in touch with a local PR firm and get some advice from them. They can tell you what will work best, and can give you some ideas of the costs involved.

Your Sales Forecast

If you have collected enough information on your field and those who work in it, you should have an idea of what you might expect to bill early on, and some possible projections of revenues based on the growth you are planning for.

Grace W. Weinstein, a financial writer and consultant whom you will meet in chapter 6, suggests that you include two revenue projections in your business plan—if possible, projections for the first year (essential), and, if you feel comfortable doing so, for five years out. One states the numbers you are reasonably confident of, those you should be able to obtain given your strategy and current market conditions. The second she calls a worst-case scenario. "This," she says, "is the least amount of revenue you're sure you can produce in the first year of business. In doing this calculation, consider all the possible pitfalls you may encounter. What if your primary client goes out of business? If this should happen, could your business survive? If not, if you don't have enough reserves to weather such a setback, this may be the time to bail out. Having a cut-and-dried number in mind at the outset will keep you from fooling yourself, wasting both money and time in an attempt to keep your business alive when it's no longer possible."

If you are working with an accountant to prepare your business plan, she will probably talk about profit and loss projections, break-even points, and projected cash-flow statements. This, with an accountant's help, puts a much finer point on your business plan. After creating the simple plan I am discussing here, you may want to get help from a professional. This initial plan will be a big help right from the start.

Your Operating Plan

Your operating plan will start to pull things together. It should include details on how and where you plan to work, how you might work with others, the legal structure of your company, and your policies regarding payments, credit, and collections. It's sort of the driver's manual of your business (except that yours will probably be better than the one that came with a car I had a few years ago).

Here are a few of the topics that are especially meaningful for a consulting business:

The Home Space You Will Need

The typical solo consultant operating from a home office really doesn't need much space. More than working space, the real need is usually for storage. As your practice grows, you will need more storage for the paperwork you generate. If much of that material arrived as digital data, you should be able to either store it on your computer or burn discs that will give you permanent records. I'd strongly urge you to keep data you don't have to access on discs and to locate them away from your home office. If I tried to store all the research and manuscripts of the books I've written over the past thirty years, I'd probably need several garages; instead, all of

Home Office Tip . . .

If you are really cramped for storage space, or you would like to have your data in several safe places, consider some of the online storage sites. For very little money you can have online access to data storage that could otherwise be damaged or lost due to the usual problems you might encounter in your home office.

the manuscripts are on individual discs that take up about as much space as two shoe boxes, and they are stored away from my home office.

You will probably begin with just the necessities: a desk, some files, and whatever equipment is appropriate for your practice. But this is the time to think about what you will need as you grow, and to outline it in your business plan.

If any special construction will be needed, such as a separate door, include it in your plan. If there will be any special wiring for phone lines, power, and computer connections, include this in your plan. If you are planning to use your garage for record storage, think about having closets or chests built that are airtight and insulated, and maybe even fireproof. Most garages are unheated, and changes in temperature and humidity can destroy paper and computer discs before you know it. Security should be considered as well.

Once you have a clear picture of what will go into your home office, begin to get all the costs together. You will need these figures later when we get to a description of your financial planning. Typical figures include:

- Rent or mortgage payments
- Utilities—heat, electricity, telephone, water, Internet connection, and whatever else will be part of your operation
- Insurance
- Any costs necessary to turn that spare room (or closet) into a functional office space

Legal Requirements

Whether you plan to incorporate, set up a limited liability corporation, or operate as a sole proprietor, you will need some legal advice. Depending on your location, you may need special licenses or permits. And the use of your home may require getting an exception from one of the many local zoning ordinances that towns are so fond of enacting. There may even be some special insurance needed in order to comply with some of these ordinances. Start thinking about what you may need before you read chapters 8 and 9.

If you plan to have others working from your home office, whether full-time or part-time, there can be some pretty rigorous conditions you may have to meet (for example, a separate bathroom). You will have to get the specs from your town's local building authority.

Credit and Collection Policies

Unless you are selling some products that relate to your regular consulting services, chances are that all you will be billing for is time spent on a client's behalf, or work in progress based on agreements you have made with clients.

Now is the time to decide how frequently you will bill your clients. Here are some of the considerations important to most consultancies:

- Will you be asking for advance payments prior to beginning work on a project?
- How will you check the credit and payment history of potential clients?
- If a potential client fails to measure up to your credit guidelines, are you willing to make exceptions? How far out on a limb are you willing to go?
- What are your plans for continuing work on a project when a client fails to make a timely progress payment?
- Will you have a "kill fee"—a fee the client must agree to pay if the assignment is canceled after a certain amount of work has been done?
- Will you accept payment by credit cards?

Chapter 6 covers these and other financial issues, but you should be able to answer most of these questions at this point.

Structure and Management

Unless you are planning to incorporate and work either with salaried employees, part-timers, or strategic alliances with other professionals, this portion of your business plan will be pretty straightforward: You will be doing everything. In any case, you should think about who might take over the business if you were to become disabled or even die.

If you are incorporating, you will have a board of directors, and this is the place to identify them, their duties, and all contact information. Regardless of whether you are planning to operate as a sole proprietor or to go full bore with a corporate format, this section should include the names and contact information of your attorney, accountant, banker, insurance agent(s), and others who might play some role in your business.

Relevant Financial Statements

If you are incorporating, you should have financial statements from all others who will have an active role and some ownership in your company. If you are going it alone, your own personal financial statement should be part of your business plan. This section is especially important if you will be seeking capital from banks or other lending institutions.

Capitalization

At this point, some guesswork will be needed. You should have a good idea of what most of your fixed expenses will be, since you will be operating from a home office. However, even small start-up consultancies have a way of costing more to run than the owner initially anticipates. Some will tell you that you should expand every expense line item by a fixed amount (the suggestions vary from 10 percent to 20 percent). Others will tell you that adding fixed amounts to every line item distorts the overall start-up picture. Those who take this view claim that it's best to have a separate line item for all contingencies. I tend to agree with this. I think it's better to have a realistic capitalization figure, yet be prepared to deal with variations independently.

If you are incorporating and you have investors lined up, this is where you should describe the relationship, the amounts they are contributing, and the number of shares they will own for their investment.

Other Items That Can Be Included in Your Business Plan

Most business plans include a detailed financial plan at this point. Chapter 6 covers the details of this portion of your business plan, including such things as a profit and loss projection of your first year in business, a projected cash-flow analysis, and a break-even analysis.

Depending on your special needs, here are a few other items that you might want to include in your business plan:

- Studies, special reports, and relevant articles that relate to your field
- A complete list of all the equipment you already have and that which you plan to buy, including any supplies that this equipment might require on a regular basis
- Any agreements, leases, and contracts that relate to your business and its home office location
- Lists of prospects, letters of endorsement, certificates, awards, and licenses needed to operate your business
- Magazine and journal articles relevant to your start-up

Sources of Capital

If you are planning to seek capital beyond that which you already have to start your business, this is the place to itemize the sources you plan to use and the amounts that you anticipate needing. It's more than likely you will be seeking investment capital from private sources rather than from banks and other lending institutions. It's not easy to get start-up capital from banks and other commercial sources, mainly because there is probably little you can offer as collateral for the loan (or loans). So, for private investors, you should include details on the following:

- The amount of money needed to open the business and survive for the first year
- The amount of money you might need over a longer period of time, usually figured at five years, for operating capital as well as money to use on growth and business development
- A clear description of how you anticipate using the borrowed money
- An estimate on what return the lender might expect on his or her investment
- A plan to pay back loans, including agreed-upon interest rates
- A plan to share ownership of the business with any of the investors
- A statement outlining what voice, if any, investors will have in the management of your company
- A plan for regular financial reporting to the investors

That's About It

I have avoided giving you a strict layout to follow. If you need this kind of help, it's available from the U.S. Small Business Administration (www.sba.gov) and other sources, such as the Service Corps of Retired Executives (www.score.org), along with most commercial publishers that have books and pamphlets on the subject. I outlined this material in a narrative form mainly because I wanted to set you thinking about your business rather than just filling in boxes. There's nothing wrong with using defined forms, except that I have yet to find any that work for all businesses. If what you have just read has got you thinking and has led you to gather what you think you will need, then you can do your own plan (or at the very least, you will have everything in hand when you use one of the many systems available).

Frequently Asked Questions

1. *Can I skip the business plan? I already have clients signed up, I don't need investor capital, and my home office is ready to go.*

    I would advise against skipping the business plan. However, there's no reason why you have to slavishly do everything I have suggested if it's already in place. Just provide the information that's needed. Even though you may think you have everything you need and have all the answers, I strongly suggest that you review what you have in terms of what has been outlined in this chapter.

2. *It seems like it could take a lot of time to create a successful business plan. How long should it take to do one for a typical home-based consulting business?*

    If you have all the information at your fingertips and in your files, it should only take a few days. However, the writing of the plan is the easy part. The difficult part is asking the right questions and then gathering the information you need to answer these questions. To do it right, I'd suggest you assume that it will take at least two or three weeks. You may be in a position to work on your plan full-time, but if you will be doing it in your spare time, I'd suggest that you do it by gathering all the information you need first and then answering the questions before you start writing. Really, the writing is the easy part.

05

Making Your Move

So far, I've talked mainly about the details that everyone must deal with when starting a home-based consulting business. The licenses, the skills needed, the legal factors, financing—all the real-world issues. Now you are at the point where the decision gets personal. If you have never been your own boss or haven't worked in situations where certain personal skills are important, it's time to see if you have what it takes. It's time to see if you have the ability to manage your time a lot differently than the way you may have been doing it while working for someone else. It's time to see if the skills you have learned and honed over the years can be used effectively, or modified sufficiently to ensure success as a self-employed consultant. And, it's time for you to get a clear picture of your decision-making skills. These are the skills that, in addition to those of your chosen profession, will be most needed to succeed on your own.

The transition from being employed by someone else to working for yourself is a dramatic one, especially if you have been working for someone else for most of your working life. As dramatic, or possibly even traumatic, as it may seem, the transition from employee to being self-employed takes a lot less time than it took for you to get up and running when you first entered the world of work. Remember that this time you are bringing skills and accomplishments that can be brought to bear on clients' assignments immediately. And remember that you have been through the mill, so to speak, when it comes to knowing how people in your field interact and react to each other. It's not like going from college to your first job; it's like going from one job to another—except that this time you are in charge of you. That's what this chapter is all about.

Your Skills and Your Ability to Use Them

Most of the skills we learn are transferable from one situation to another. If, for example, you can express an idea to a group of your present peers, you have the basics you will need for a consulting career. All you need to know is what different groups are looking for when they seek information from you. The skill of setting goals is the same for a management consultant as it is for someone consulting on chemical processing. Only the subject matter is different. We are all a lot more flexible than we think. We tend to limit ourselves because of subject specialties we have mastered, but an important ability for all aspects of life is being adaptable. Marc Dorio, the psychologist and management consultant you met earlier, explains that there are essentially five major skill sets that are critical for success in most consulting situations. They are:

- Research and forecasting
- Communicating in the appropriate media
- Organizing and leading
- Human relations
- The basic skills needed in all work situations

"The skills required to be successful as an employee are pretty much the same as those required to be a successful consultant," Dorio explains. "The real test that anyone who works faces is his or her flexibility and adaptability in a variety of situations. For example, communicating ideas to fellow workers as an employee is not much different than trying to explain the same ideas to a group of clients when you are working as an independent consultant. The flexibility lies in how you see yourself in relation to the individuals in each group, how you perceive their needs, and how critical it is for them to accept what you are saying."

What follows are Marc's suggestions for some basic self-analysis anyone contemplating working from a home-based consulting firm can use.

Research and Forecasting Skills

Most consulting assignments involve solving problems that clients think they may have identified. According to Dorio, client-identified problems are merely the tip of the iceberg. "The real task," he explains, "is getting beneath and beyond the problem the clients thinks he or she has and to identify the underlying problems and issues. It's like a chess game; you can never win if you only think one move ahead."

You may have mastered these skills in the narrow confines of a job you have done for years, but now the real task is to make use of these skills in the much wider and often more demanding environment of consulting with a variety of different clients. "It's the consultants with a one-answer-fits-all approach who are going to have difficulty," Dorio explains.

Information collection is a skill that every consultant must master. It's not simply knowing where to look for the material needed—it's also having the ability to do it quickly and accurately in a variety of different situations. Successful consultants must not only be able to locate the information, but also know how to draw from masses of data to find the answers that will be relevant and important to their clients.

The ability to see and consider a wide range of possible solutions to a problem is a key characteristic for success in consulting. Even when you are pressed for answers, you must be able to see all—or, at least most—of the possible alternatives clearly and be able to explain the benefits and drawbacks of each to your clients. Unfortunately, this can often lead clients to feel that their consultants are avoiding the decision-making process. "Too many clients assume that there is only one way to solve a problem," Dorio says, "and when you present alternatives, you can be seen as waffling. The best way to avoid this issue is to rank-order, if you can, the chances of success of each of the alternatives. This kind of thinking is seldom appreciated within companies, but it is critical for consultants to provide it. All you may have learned about analyzing information and presenting it appropriately in a corporate setting will provide the groundwork you need to do the best possible work you can for your clients."

Dorio explains that the skills needed to identify problems, set goals, search out resources, and analyze strategies are typically learned on the job. However, he adds, "These abilities are usually learned and mastered in the narrow context of the work done for an employer. The real test comes when a person who worked in one field can tap the core elements of each and transfer them to other situations that he or she may encounter in any given client consultation." This notion of *skill transfer* is a major field of study in psychology, but it's easy enough to understand without any extensive study if you think of it simply as the ability to use skills you have learned in one field when analyzing situations in other fields. You have probably not faced something like this if you have worked mainly in one field, but you can set your comfort zone if you see yourself as being pretty flexible, and seldom willing to settle for the first solution to a problem that jumps to mind.

Communication Skills

Being able to communicate in a variety of media is a critical skill needed for success in consulting. You may be asked to submit your report in writing or asked to present your findings and suggestions to a group. You may even be asked to deliver your solutions via a closed-circuit broadcast to the client's staff and affiliates all around the world. Fortunately, most communication skills are readily transferable from one field to another. Whether it's writing, speaking, or listening, you should have few problems transferring what you have mastered from one field to another.

Where you might encounter problems is with the different aspects of using these tools. For example, expressing your ideas verbally to a group of engineers will require a different focus than you might use when addressing a group of sales managers. Engineers and scientists will look for precision, well-thought-out arguments, and the ability to present what you know in a fully logical way. You might find that sales and marketing people are less interested in the underlying reasoning for your solutions and more interested in your getting to the point quickly. Your skill at persuading will transfer to any situation, but how you do it will be the test of your flexibility. Just for grins, think about how you would persuade a group of engineers and a group of field sales managers that your plan to drastically modify the company line was going to make the difference between the success or failure of a recent acquisition.

Few people think of listening when the subject of communication is mentioned. They only think of how they will make their views known to others. However, the way you listen is just as important as what you say and how you say it. It's not just listening; it's listening intently and evaluating what you hear. If you are accustomed to tuning out most of what you hear from your current company's windbag

> **Consultant's Tip . . .**
>
> A good consultant can gather information with a simple nod, an occasional *aha*, and even a long and seemingly deep *ummmmmmm*. After all, it will be difficult to help anyone unless you have all the facts you need. And, in most cases, these facts will be gathered in face-to-face meetings, not from printed reports. These nondirective conversations are critical for success in any consulting situation.

executives, you will definitely have to sharpen your listening skills for your new venture as a consultant. Consultants, like psychologists, must master the ability of listening to what is being said as well as what is *not* being said. What is not being said can sometimes be inferred from the speaker's presentation and body language.

Test yourself: Do you frequently interrupt someone to interject your thoughts on the subject being discussed? If you do, you need to curb the impulse. Do you tend to ask specific questions during a conversation? If you do, curb the impulse and ask them later. In the meantime, try a nondirective approach with something like, "Tell me more about that." Just encourage the other person to talk—and then listen, listen, and listen some more.

Organizational and Leadership Skills

The critical skill here is the ability to lead without forcing people to do what you want them to do. The goal is to get them to want what you want, and to encourage them to make it happen.

How good are you at coaching, teaching, and getting others to help you willingly? How about delegating responsibility and managing conflict? These are all skills that are needed for success, whether you remain employed by someone else, or strike out on your own. However, they are especially important when you are on your own and working with clients.

An especially important skill is the ability to present, explain, and sell new and often difficult ideas to others. It's a skill successful salespeople usually learn early in their careers. However, those whose work is more limited to support functions seldom get the opportunity to master these skills. If you feel you need some help in this area, see what courses might be available in any of the continuing education programs offered by local schools and service organizations.

Many consultants find themselves providing counseling services that they were never prepared for by any previous work experience. This is what most human resource consultants do, but it's seldom in the bag of tricks of the engineer or manufacturing consultant. But there are times when even those whose work might be thought to be technical are called on to deal with individuals as they relate to some technical program. Most of the major national scientific and technical associations offer on-site or even distance-learning training programs that are worth considering.

Managing conflict is an activity that all consultants find themselves involved in from time to time. When your recommendation as a consultant provides support for one group within a company, you may encounter hostility from another. It may be your responsibility to resolve these issues. New engineering consultants often complain that they never thought this would be part of the package. While they see themselves as providing technical and scientific support, they seldom envision that it could become their responsibility to resolve the conflict engendered by their recommendations.

Consultants often find themselves coaching and counseling their clients, or the employees of their clients. These skills are used mainly to get people on board when your client has agreed to your suggestions and plans. You will probably be asked to "sell" the plan to those who will have to implement it. This often involves teaching, training, and coordinating the entire process. You don't have to have special training in teaching, but you should feel comfortable in the role and be able to lead both individuals and groups.

An ability to delegate responsibility is also very helpful. If your project involves large groups, it might be necessary to identify appropriate people in the groups and to delegate the work they need to do to implement the plan your client has agreed to.

Human Relations Skills

A lot of what has already been said could be described as human relations skills, but in this area you could see yourself more in one-on-one situations, rather than in group situations. Typical consulting assignments usually involve individual interaction as well as working with groups. Chances are that most of your initial client meetings, including the pitch, will involve one or only a few people.

A good consultant, like a good psychologist, is a careful listener. You will have your chance to talk, but the ability to build rapport with the people you work with is critical for success. You may have the best ideas in the world, but if you cannot connect with the people who want and need them, you will have difficulty being a consultant.

It is critically important to always be sensitive to the needs and interests of your clients. You need to know a lot more about each person than just the details of the project you've been engaged to work on. Early on you should be able to detect which individuals you interact with are supportive of your ideas, and which individuals are not. And you should be able to respond with equal enthusiasm to all, regardless of where you stand, relative to the views of the others. Neutrality is not an easy skill to acquire, and you have to work at it. If any of the people on the client side sense a bias, you will be in trouble.

Two of the toughest traits to acquire are the willingness to share credit when credit is due, and the ability to accept blame when it's deserved. It sure is tempting to say to a client, "There, I told you so!" But if you want another assignment, you better be able to let the client think that much of the success of the idea was his or hers in the first place. It's also tempting to tell other clients how poorly managed one of your earlier clients was until you were hired. The best advice I can give you here is to

Can You Deal Calmly with Hostility?

You may find yourself having to support the ideas of one member of a client team in the face of hostility from others. The key to success in this case is to do so without making it personal. Stick to the facts, respond to criticism neutrally, and lead the others to change their minds, rather than trying to tell them that they have to change their minds. If you ever have a chance to see the film *Twelve Angry Men (1957)*, take it. In fact, watch it several times. In this film, eleven jurors agree to convict someone of a capital crime while one lone juror holds out. It's the interplay of the jurors that is fascinating and very enlightening. Watch how the lone juror, faced with intense hostility, slowly wins over the others until all eleven finally change their minds. Listen carefully to the dialogue. Watch the responses of the jurors to the comments of all the others. It's an oldie, but it's available at most video rental stores and through Netflix (and a television remake was done in 1997).

curb your enthusiasm. It's seldom a problem to get happy clients to vouch for you, but you should never tell tales out of school.

There will be times when you will have to be assertive, and it's important to avoid being personal when this is called for. It's always better to line up support from individuals you can count on before making a strong stand.

Basic Skills Needed in All Consulting Situations

So far, I have tried to identify the skills that are most needed by consultants. The following skills are just as important, but probably don't need any explanation if you have been working for even a few years in the field in which you plan to consult.

- The ability to cooperate with people you might disagree with
- The ability to manage your own time effectively and to see that your colleagues don't waste their time
- The ability to make decisions based on facts, not emotions, and the ability to enforce them without getting personal
- The ability to make schedules, adhere to them, and ensure that others don't drop the ball
- The ability to manage complex details and to direct the work of others who are responsible for any of the tasks
- The ability to set your own goals and the goals of others involved in a project
- The ability to accept responsibility and to delegate it to others
- The ability to ask for help when it's needed
- The ability to graciously accept responsibility for failure as well as success

Marc Dorio explains that he views every new consulting assignment as he would see taking a new job. "You have to look at consulting as though you are constantly changing jobs," Dorio says. "When you work for one company for any length of time, you internalize most of the routine, and after a while you have a pretty good idea of what to look for as different situations present themselves. However, as a consultant, even when I have worked with the client many times, I try to see new assignments by the company the same way I'd see walking into a brand-new job. Since you are not on the job 24/7, you don't see everything, and even when you are deeply involved with a client, you are only seeing a limited aspect of the overall operation. So, bringing a fresh perspective to each engagement, I think, is critical to doing your best work for any client."

One of the toughest transitions to make as a new consultant is to adopt Marc's point of view. One way to test your ability to do this is to envision just how you might solve a problem facing your current employer. Try to imagine how you would address the issues—not as the employee you currently are, but as someone coming to the situation without your background. You will surely have a different perspective. Now think about why you see it one way as an employee and another as a consultant.

Your view as an employee is more than likely colored by your view of what others in the company might expect you to say. And your view would also be tinged with an element of self-protection. It's hard to tell the emperor that he has no clothes when the emperor pays you a regular salary. But when you have been brought in by a naked emperor and discover that you must tell him that he is undressed, can you do it? How would you do it?

These are some of the questions that consultants face with just about every engagement. You will probably know when you've been brought in to confirm that the emperor is, in fact, without clothes, and that you are expected to go along with the charade. Can you do it? Should you do it? If you are capable of critical analysis and have the human relations skills I have been addressing so far, you should do very well as a consultant. There are times when the emperor must be made aware of his failings and it's the task of an impartial consultant to tell the truth.

Your Ability to Accomplish More Than You Ever Thought You Possibly Could

If there is one thing all consultants in all fields seem to agree on, it's that they either had the ability to manage time well when they started out, or they learned how to do it very quickly in their new career. The ability to make the most productive use of your time is as important as your ability to provide excellent services. Everyone who has had at least two jobs knows that time is mainly a local factor. Work for company A, and you may be expected to complete a task in a day that another company may give you a week to do. The work doesn't change; what changes is the perception of the time it takes to do the job.

The issue of time management has been covered more thoroughly in books and magazine articles than any other management subject. I'll leave it up to you to discover which of the many systems you choose to use, if any. It has always been my feeling that going through all the formal structures of self-management has done

Meet C. Northcote Parkinson

Parkinson made his mark in a humorous essay that was first published in *The Economist* in 1955. Parkinson was doing a tongue-in-cheek parody of his long career in the British Civil Service. He wryly pointed out, "Work expands so to fill the time available for its completion." Parkinson may have been making fun of the British Civil Service, but he was deadly serious in the point he made, and the corollaries others have proposed to his dictum. Of the others, one Edward A. Murphy is credited with some equally relevant observations. These two about time and its use are most often quoted when the subject is time: "The first 90 percent of a project takes 90 percent of the time, and the last 10 percent takes at least twice as long." Murphy's law of corporate planning states: "Anything that can be changed will be changed until there is no time left to really plan anything."

Every management consultant in the world starts out thinking that he or she can repeal these laws. But Murphy himself is credited with saying, "If anything can go wrong, it will." Of course the obvious and ironic corollary to this is, "Murphy was an optimist." Anyway, the point here is that your ability to manage your own time, and that of your clients, is critically important to your success as a consultant.

nothing more for me than add time to my work rather than to reduce the load. If making lists and checking them twice is something you are comfortable with, then I urge you to do it. It's important to do whatever works best for you, rather than to feel that there is only one way to get a grip on runaway time—especially when you charge for it, and the time you spend on some projects doesn't always result in billable hours.

By the way, I'm not the only one who avoids checklists and the more rigid rules of time management. I asked several of my clients, mainly those I know who have been especially productive, how they manage their time. What they told me is pretty much what I have been doing intuitively. Again, if you need something more structured, check out the systems that are available in many good books on time management, or sign up for a time management course.

In general, here is what has worked for me:

Set Your Priorities for Tomorrow at the End of Each Day

At the end of each work day, you know what you have accomplished and what you never got to, and your priorities for each are usually pretty clear. Make a list of what still remains to be done that was not accomplished during this day, and make a list of what needs to be done the next day. Don't waste your time trying to analyze anything; just make the simplest and most concise lists you can and call it a day.

It's far better to enter the office in the morning with a clear list of what has to be done that day than it is to try to reconstruct the previous day in order to set up your present work day. I tend to keep two lists: one containing things that must be done, and the other describing activities I'd like to address if time permits (but it won't be a problem if they are not completed).

I have met people who make their lists on one of those large calendar-type appointment books that have room for notes. And I have met others who do their to-do listing more formally on their computer. There are some good computer-based day planners that seem to have been made with this approach in mind. Check them out. I tend to do my list on whatever is available to write on, and it's about the only time I have a pencil in my hand all day. I have not seen the need to get formal and use my computer yet. More often than not, large Post-its do the job nicely for me. Stuck to my computer screen before I shut down for the day, they are the first things I see when I open my home office the next day.

Go with the Flow

Not every job on your list needs to be accomplished immediately, and many of your projects can usually be arranged just about any way you want. Everyone knows that we look forward to some projects each day and don't look forward to others. Do what seems most attractive to you first and work up to the stuff you don't especially

---

Murphy, Yet Again . . .

"Whenever you start to do something, you quickly realize that something else must be done first."

"If you don't really have to do it, and if doing it doesn't really matter, it will go perfectly every time."

want to do. No, this not a license to put off paying bills forever, but once you get your day started and your work rhythms and biorhythms seem to be in sync, it's usually easier, and often smarter, to tackle the jobs that have less appeal for you. It's like priming a pump; once you have the water in motion, the pump handle moves with a lot less effort.

I have met people who claim that just the opposite works best for them. Their idea is to get the junk work out of the way first so they can settle into a day of working on more pleasant projects. If this is what works best for you, go with it. We are all different, and being flexible is far more important than trying to force something unpleasant on yourself.

Not Everything Has to Be Planned For

Most consultants agree that their typical work day involves working on one or two major projects and in attending to maybe dozens of small tasks. Most of the less important things include activities like returning a routine phone call, ordering office supplies, getting multiple copies made of reports you plan to send to clients. The list seems endless, but I'm sure you know what I'm talking about. In most cases these small tasks don't require much (or any) thought; they are just chores that must be done. Needless to say, you will waste a lot of time if you include all this effluvia in your daily to-do list. But, if you can fit some of them in between bigger jobs, you will not only save time, but you will also discover that they often provide a decompression period between bigger and more demanding projects. Jumping from writing a chapter in a book to doing your financial planning for the next quarter without plugging in a simple transitional project is not the best way to spend your day.

If you have no little things to do and you are planning to move from one heavy project to another, take a break first. Listen to some music. Warm that cup of coffee you brought from the kitchen first thing and never got to drink. Take a break!

One of the most destructive habits we all have is failing to return to a task when we've been interrupted in order to deal with some immediate issue. We usually realize what we are doing, but rationalize not returning to the interrupted task by telling ourselves that we will do it later. This leaves a wake of small, uncompleted tasks that will bug you when you should be doing something more important. There is nothing better than clean decks when you sit down to dig into a complex issue. Finding yourself thinking about some insignificant task in the middle of a major project is extremely counterproductive.

Maintain a Consistent Flow to Your Work

A consultant's typical day is usually made up of focused office work on a client project, and all the other stuff that has to be done to keep things moving. If you find that you concentrate better in the morning, assign this period to the work you are doing that requires good focus.

Set Time Limits for the Things You Do

Once you get into the rhythm of working in your home office, you will begin to see that certain jobs can usually be accomplished in pretty much the same time every time you do them. Don't be obsessive about this, but if you mentally tell yourself that certain tasks will take fifteen minutes, try to beat that by shooting for completion in ten minutes. It can become a game, just like trying to beat your time for jogging a mile. We all tend to habituate—to assume that writing a press release is going to take an hour—so we do it in an hour when we might really be able to do it in half an hour.

Working from Home Is Very Different from Working with Others

It's a cliché, but many self-employed consultants who work from home offices will tell you that they work for the worst bosses in the world—themselves. This includes those who see themselves as slave drivers, never satisfied with their performance, as well as those softies who make every excuse in the book for poor performance. Which one are you?

Any good book on people management will help you. Whatever the system tells you to do when managing others is what you should do when you manage yourself. In simplest terms, feel free to reward yourself for work well done, and to invoke some predetermined disincentive for work that you messed up. It's basic psychology—rewards and inhibitors—except that you are playing all the roles yourself.

One trick you can use is to set specific rewards in advance so you have something to shoot for. Tell yourself that if you finish a client report by 4:30, you will close up shop early and go to that movie you especially wanted to see. Fail to meet the deadline you've set, and you must skip a TV show you wanted to watch that evening. Vague goals have no real strength. Specific goals do.

How Do You Shape Up So Far?

If you have gotten this far, it's safe to assume that you are more than casually interested in working as a consultant from a home office. I've thrown a lot at you; some of it may be intimidating, while some of it may seem like a blinding glimpse of the obvious. However, it's all part of the overall picture of the work you are planning to do. The chapters that follow will take you from the wishful thinking phase to the planning and start-up phases.

What do you think? Is a home-based consulting business for you? Are you ready to do the financial planning, address the legal issues, and take all the other steps that could change your life? I hope so! Believe me, I only had salaried jobs for the first four years of my working life, and I've been on my own ever since. I seldom look back, but when I do, it's to say, "I learned a lot in those four years as an employee, but the most important lesson was that there is nothing like running your own show!"

Frequently Asked Questions

1. *I'm ready to do it, but should I have a fallback plan?*

   You should always have a fallback plan for every risk you take. However, don't obsess over it. Remember: You don't plan to spend your vacation in the lifeboat of a cruise ship, but it's comforting to know the lifeboats are there. The major element of a fallback plan is simply to have enough money to cover any debts you might have encountered and to cover your cost of living while you regroup and decide what to do next. If you have the skills needed to be a good consultant, and for whatever reason your business doesn't make it, you should not have much trouble getting a job again.

2. *How much time should I allow for a home-based consulting business to start turning a profit?*

   Most people will tell you that you should be able to survive for at least a year before you break even, but I'd suggest that you plan further out. There are so many different types of home-based consulting businesses that an average number is really meaningless. If you are opening the doors with business in hand, you should hit the mark earlier than you might if you were starting from scratch. See if there are any statistics for start-ups in your particular field and use this data in your planning.

06

What Are You Worth?

Unless you have worked for a consulting firm or have used the services of independent consultants before, you probably have no idea of how or what to charge for your services. Or, you may have picked up an idea that, if used, will not exactly get you off to a roaring start. There is and always has been a lot of scuttlebutt among consultants about fees and charges. Despite all the rumors, rumors of rumors, and just plain misinformation, most consultants' fees seem to hover in the same ballpark. But remember—different consultants play in different ballparks. Most consultants, like most baseball players, start out in the minor leagues and move up to the majors as their abilities and triumphs are recognized. And again, not unlike baseball players, the money grows proportionally.

I have to assume a starting point, so what follows is an outline of what a new and inexperienced consultant would face and do in terms of pricing and financial management from square one. Even if you have had some experience and exposure to consulting and the pricing of consulting services, you might not want to skip this chapter. Old dogs can usually learn new tricks!

If there's any single mistake new consultants make, it's to check out what their established competitors charge and either meet them dollar for dollar, or price their services slightly lower to attract the clients whose interest is based more on economy than on wanting the best possible services. It is, of course, good policy to make sure you are neither too low nor too high, but this doesn't take into account any of your operating costs and the profit you should make on your invested capital. And, it fails to recognize that you are selling a professional service, not vegetables off a cart.

Most research I have seen recently indicates that a consultant whose price is too low is seldom seen to be the better choice. Does this mean that you should open your doors and price your services way above your competitors? It could. For now, however, let's look at pricing consulting services in the most realistic terms: those that will gain you entry to the business and allow you to get established with a minimum of risk.

The Basic Pricing Formula

You do have a product to sell. It's not something you can make in advance and ship to customers when you get orders, but it's still a product: your knowledge, education, and experience. Although it may seem to amount to a few bucks' worth of paper and binders that the client gets, it's what's between the covers of your client report that your client is paying for.

It's common practice for many who write about the consulting business to draw deep lines in the sand between products and services. This is a mistake, mainly because a lot of research and experience with the pricing and marketing of products has currency in the field of selling intangibles, such as consulting services. The major difference, of course, is that the product of a consulting assignment is made to order. It's the result of an effort totally unlike that of producing any other products. This doesn't change the fact that a consultant's work and reports can be thought of as products for the purpose of pricing. After that, do whatever you feel is necessary to maintain the image you see of yourself and your consulting work.

All this boils down to three notions which you must consider when you decide what to charge for each of the services you will perform. Here they are:

1. No matter what others charge, no matter what you hear on the street, your fees can only be as high as your prospective clients are willing to pay. You may be worth every penny of the megabucks per hour you could have gotten in Gotham City, but in East Flatmattress, your fees will be lower.

2. Your fees will also be determined by the number of clients in your area and your ability to serve them consistently. If you have a big reputation and you and your clients can afford for you to commute from your beach home on Nantucket to see them, you will be living every consultant's dream. If you are just starting out, make sure there is sufficient business in your area to get you started. Don't make the mistake of starting with the one major client in your area if there is little or no potential for other business. Sooner or later you will have a competitor for that one client.

3. Don't think of your fee as your income. Your income is your fee less all your fixed and variable expenses. You must think of yourself as a business, which is responsible for providing you with an income. This may seem like splitting hairs, but it will avoid a lot of possible disasters if you get used to the fact that your fee is not your personal income. Of course, it could be if your spouse picks up all the expenses. If you are in that situation, consider becoming a world-class surfer; don't bother with consulting.

I won't list all of the expenses you will have, even when operating from a home office. Most of them are nickels and dimes, but even pocket change turns into real money quicker than you may think. Some of them, however, will eat you alive unless you watch them. Telephone bills, equipment rental and service, furniture and storage, and taxes, taxes, taxes; this last expense alone will help you see that your fee is not going to be your income.

Most new consultants like to point out that at least they don't have the expense of carrying an inventory of products. That glee usually vanishes quickly when I tell them that they have something worse than inventory to worry about. At least inventory has a market value. What is worse than having inventory? It's having to spend time on things that won't produce income. Your billable hours seldom include the time you spend in new business development, proposal writing, and all the office chores you would assign to someone else if you could afford it. No matter how you decide to bill clients for your work, you will end up measuring your successes by some unit of time. And, to invoke another cliché, time is money.

A Typical Example

Here's a typical situation, based on Base 10 math so you can visualize it without having to turn on your calculator or count on your fingers. You have decided that $100 might be an appropriate hourly rate. You plan to work the usual forty-hour week. This translates to a need to produce $4,000 of weekly gross income. Not bad—an annual income of $200,000. However, most consultants I've talked with tell me that only about half of their typical week is devoted to doing work that can be legitimately billed. So, your gross income has just been reduced by half.

Now, add up all your estimated expenses. Just for the purpose of this exercise, suppose that you foresee average monthly expenses of $4,000, or $48,000 a year. Your personal income has just been reduced to $52,000. Not exactly a stellar figure, but it makes my point: Start with a realistic estimate of what your expenses will be and work backward to determine how your fees will be determined. You may find that you will be able to work fewer hours than you expected on nonbillable chores and have enough going for you so that you spend more than half your time on work which can be billed to a client.

Now, let's take this same situation and see what the number really should be. Assume that you would like to show a $100,000 personal income, and that your expenses would be the same, and that the time spent on billable work will be the same; what would your hourly fee have to be? Your gross billing would have to be $248,000. Assuming a fifty-week work year, and a forty-hour work week, you would have to set your fee at $124 per hour. This is a reasonable number, even for a beginning consultant, and not significantly more than the $100 an hour you had been contemplating.

But this isn't the end of the exercise. What we have just done is to compute what you need to cover the personal income you want and to cover your anticipated expenses. But, it doesn't cover profit, and it doesn't cover the possibility that you may actually earn less than you anticipate. Now you are at the point where you begin to consider what the market will bear, and you see what your competitors are charging. If you are way out of line, you may have to adjust your planned expenses, possibly by canceling that order for the new BMW you thought you just might buy. More than likely, however, you will see that minor adjustments will probably put you within 10 or 15 percent of what your competitors are charging, and that's a pretty safe place to be.

There are more sophisticated equations you can use, and most of them are based on calculating overhead numbers for yourself and anyone else who might work for you. Overhead varies dramatically from year to year, as we see quite dramatically in times of economic instability. So my best advice is to work with current numbers, but account for them by using historical averages to plan for the future.

How to Get Those Competitive Numbers

If you already know some of the consultants working in your area, I'm sure some would be willing to give you at least some ballpark numbers. But remember, no matter how friendly they may be, you will be competing for some of the same business. You may be able to get some figures from those who hire consultants, but the most reliable sources will probably be trade and professional associations in your geographical area that track these numbers in your field.

If there are any temp agencies or companies that specialize in subcontracting work in your field, see what they charge for their services. Check the employment advertising in your area and see what companies might be paying their employees for the work you propose to do on a consulting basis.

The Internet is one of the best sources of information, although some of it can be misleading. When you can validate the source, you should be able to dig up the numbers you need from a wide variety of Web sites. Local, state, and federal agencies that report on your industry might be able to give you what you need.

If all else fails, you can do what one consultant friend of mine did many years ago. He told me that everyone was closemouthed in his area, and although the statistics he needed were available online, the most recent figures were already five years old. Since there was a fairly large number of companies that could use his services, he decided to go with his best fee guesstimate and test-market his fledgling consultancy with a few clients to see what would fly. He was pleasantly surprised to learn from one client who took him on that he was slightly lower than most of his competitors. He hadn't planned on starting out by underbidding competitors, but his test-marketing approach led him to charge the going rate once he opened his doors for full-time business. Most people who start consulting on a part-time basis learn what the appropriate rates are without having to take major risks.

The Many Ways of Charging for Your Services

Those new to consulting sometimes lament the lack of a "standard" way to charge for consulting services. Once they understand all the variables involved, and the benefits and drawbacks of each, they see that a one-way-fits-all approach just isn't practical. It's not uncommon for consultants dealing with people in different divisions of the same corporation to charge one by the job, another by the hour, and yet another by the use of a retainer. The way you charge should be determined with each assignment—unless, of course, you have a series of similar assignments for a client where the chosen formula works for all assignments.

Regardless of how you choose to bill for specific services, there are several issues you need to resolve about your overall approach to pricing.

Introductory Pricing

The idea of a special price to get a foot in the door is not uncommon, but it has its pitfalls. Doing this, some claim, sets up a price-level expectancy, and it's not easy to raise the client to the level you have been charging others. Some feel that introductory discounts cheapen the perceived value of the service offered. As one consultant put it, "You don't sell professional services the same way you sell retail products." It's hard to take an absolute stand on this issue. Whether you use introductory pricing or not is usually based on the amount and quality of your entrenched competition. Using deep discounts to steal business is, without question, morally wrong, and just not the kind of behavior expected of consultants who are providing professional services.

Competitive Pricing

Most consultants are reluctant to chip away at their competitors by lowering their fees in order to bring in more work. The better consultants prefer to compete on the basis of the quality of their work, not on cutting prices. New consultants are well advised to adhere to this principle. Build your name on the quality of your work and not your ability to wheel and deal, and you will earn a good reputation quickly.

Discounting

Although most consultants will tell you that they do not offer discounts, the real world often intrudes. Suppose, for example, that a major client has work that will occupy you at least two or three days a week, and this could continue for years. Would you offer the client a discount to get the work? Of course you would, and your answer does not diminish your professional reputation at all. After all, think about the time and money you might have to spend to gain the billable hours that are being offered to you. So, while you may like to say that it's not your policy to offer discounts, you should be flexible enough to see what the client has in mind.

> **The 80/20 Rule Applies to Consulting, Too**
>
> One word of caution is needed for situations where a major client offers to use you extensively: You do not want to fall into the 80/20 trap, where you get 80 percent of your business from 20 percent of your client base. The numbers are arbitrary, but I'm sure you have seen mention of the 80/20 rule in other situations. As comforting as it may seem to have three of your five days paid for regularly, it can be dangerous in that you could fail to prospect for new business. Assignments like this can go on for years, but they can also dry up very quickly, too.

Charging by the Hour

There's plenty of precedent for charging by the hour. Attorneys do it, and most consultants charge for a good many of the services they provide based on an hourly rate. It's probably the payment method most clients prefer, even though in some cases other methods might be more advantageous for them. And, if you have done the financial planning I have discussed so far, you have real numbers by which to measure your progress.

One of the major benefits of charging by the hour for you is that you will be able to charge for hours that you never anticipated when you first discussed the engagement with the client. Most clients will ask you to give them an estimate of the time you expect to spend on the project so they will have an idea of what the fee will be. This isn't unreasonable, and when you do give them the estimate, you should include a list of all the tasks you see as necessary in order to complete the assignment. However, you should also explain that anything that keeps the clock running past the estimated time will be itemized and billed.

You will discover that clients often insist that a bunch of their executives be allowed to contribute their ideas, consequently running up the hours outrageously. Suggest that your contacts be limited to only a few, with the understanding that you will have access to others if you need to talk with them. This not only tidies up the project for you, but it also ensures that you won't have to hit the client for time wasted by one of the "committee members." Incidentally, this is a good thing to do, regardless of the need to stay within budget, because it forces your client to focus.

Charging by the Job

Some clients often see charging by the hour as a license to steal, and insist on paying on a per-project basis. Regardless of how you actually bill the client, your internal standard has to be based on your hourly rate. You certainly don't have to tell the client this when he or she insists on a per-job estimate. What most clients don't realize is that when they insist on a per-project billing, the consultant not only has to work with her best guess on the time needed to complete the job, but also has to guess about what contingencies might pop up that were never considered when the assignment was first discussed. If you don't plug in a figure for unanticipated work, you will lose money.

It's impossible to give you a fudge factor that will work for all situations and projects. Once you gain enough experience in handling the type of project that a client wants billed on a per-project basis, you will have a good idea of how much to build into the quoted fee to cover unanticipated work. In most of my book ghostwriting and collaboration work, I have found it necessary to add at least 20 percent to the fee that I would anticipate getting if we had worked on an hourly basis. Others I know in the business tell me that their contingency factor is usually 30 percent.

Working on a Retainer

It's a mistake to push clients for retainer relationships just because you see the retainer as a way to stabilize your cash flow. Retainer agreements should benefit the client as well as the consultant. Typically, retainer agreements are initiated after the client and the consultant have had a long-enough relationship so that the client can predict the company's needs on a periodic basis, and the consultant can set aside specific blocks of time to accommodate those client needs. Retainer arrangements seldom go smoothly when there is considerable variation in the client's needs.

The usual retainer agreement stipulates the time the consultant is to spend with the client and the rate of payment for that time. The client is billed monthly, regardless of whether or not the time is used. Most agreements stipulate a price for time used beyond the amount contracted for. It seems popular to charge for the time used beyond the agreed-upon amount at slightly less per hour than the contracted amount. You might think of this as something akin to a volume discount. However, the problems that usually emerge with retainer agreements are those associated with billing for unused time. These issues, as you might imagine, usually

The Problems with Retainer Arrangements

Apart from the one appealing feature—a predictable income—retainer agreements have some serious drawbacks. In addition to the problem of a client packing too much work into the time allotted, there comes a time when there is far less work, but the fee goes on. This usually raises the What-have-you-done-for-me-lately question. Clients are seldom willing to acknowledge that they got more for their money earlier in the arrangement.

Then, there is the familiarity factor. After a while you may be thought of in the same terms as an in-house employee, which translates to feeling that you must jump when the command is given.

And, finally, between the time you negotiated a rate for the retainer and the time you started with the client, it could be that a major project becomes available that will require time you no longer have because of this agreement.

These are all issues that must be considered carefully when you are initially blinded by the possibility of some regular income from a retainer agreement.

occur when it isn't possible to predict a steady use of consulting time. Enter retainer agreements with care.

Contingency Agreements

It's not uncommon for clients who have not worked with consultants before to suggest payment based on whether or not the consultant's advice pans out. This is not where you want to go for a number of reasons. First of all, you will probably have absolutely no control over the way the client implements the plans, suggestions, and ideas you propose. Second, you will have no control over the environment in which the suggestions are used. And, third, unless you specifically offer to follow through with any implementation, you cannot guarantee your plan's success. After all, you are not operating in the client's business—you are in the consulting business.

I have heard of consultants agreeing to adjusted fees in return for a payment based on the success or failure of a plan. If you go that route, which I would suggest you avoid, then any bonus money should always amount to more than you would earn if the client had agreed to your full fee, up front. You are taking a risk over which you have no control. I have no solid guidelines to offer for the amount a fee could be reduced in the event of failure, but you should at least be compensated for all of your out-of-pocket expenses, plus a slight reduction in your hourly fee.

Rate Variations for Different Clients

It's not unusual for consultants to vary their fees with different clients. However, there must be a real reason for doing this, and you should be able to explain your reasons to clients, as discriminatory billing could have some litigious possibilities. Discounting your fee for your brother-in-law seems like behavior that could get you in trouble. But offering a slightly lower price to a new client doesn't seem to have any lurking legal peril. Just make sure that the client being charged the lower figure fully understands that it is an introductory offer figure, and get his acknowledgment in writing if you can. If you bill at the lower rate for an agreed-upon period of time and then revert to your standard rate, and you can document this, you should be okay.

This is one reason why some consultants suggest that quoting a fixed fee for a project is the better way to go. They surely base the quoted fee on time they will spend on the project, plus expenses. But the proposal given to the client does not contain any reference to the time that will be spent on the project. It is nearly impossible for two consultants to come up with exactly the same estimate for a project, so the time basis for comparison is not that obvious. In short, there is more maneuvering room. But, as you probably know, it's easier to lose your shirt when quoting a fixed fee than when quoting on a time basis.

What Expenses Can You Charge to Clients?

No two consultants look at this issue the same way. Lawyers tend to bill for everything, including postage and the money the telephone company charges them for individual calls. Engineering consultants usually bill for special computer time they must buy when working on some client assignments. Human resource consultants will usually bill the costs for testing materials they use in conjunction with corporate assignments. Whether you bill some expenses or not really needs to be determined by what is required by the project and what is already customary in your field.

Travel time is billed by some consultants. They reason that time spent traveling to and from a client's office is time that could have been spent working on billable projects. Again, there is no one answer that fits all situations. If it's customary in your field to bill for travel time, then you should do it. Several consultants have told me that they will bill travel time and expenses if the travel period exceeds more than four hours, and if the travel is going to be frequent enough to eat into time that would not be available to do other work. Again, industry standards should be your guideline.

Expenses are always billed at cost, and supporting invoices and receipts should always accurately document your expense billing to a client.

How to Get Start-Up Capital

Grace Weinstein says that it's often easier to find start-up capital for a candy store than a consulting business. "At least a candy store has inventory that can be sold off if the business fails, or it can be eaten," she says with tongue in cheek (or maybe even a piece of chocolate). She explains that most people rely on personal savings, credit cards, and—often—loans from family and friends to get started. Loans from relatives should be carefully structured as business deals, both to maintain the relationship and to avoid tax consequences. Some use loans obtained by pledging some form of collateral; home equity loans and lines of credit have been popular, although these sources of cash are more difficult to obtain when home values are declining. But no matter how you look at it, borrowing money to start a consulting business, or any other labor-intensive business, is not easy.

Meet Grace W. Weinstein

You met Grace briefly in chapter 4. Grace's articles have appeared in such prestigious periodicals as *The Financial Times, Wealth Manager, Financial Planning, Business Week, Kiplinger's Personal Finance, Consumer Reports, Investment Vision,* and *Working Mother.* She is the author of thirteen books, all with major publishers. She has prepared special editorial sections for *Barron's, USA Weekend, Time, Institutional Investor,* and many other periodicals. Grace has been a member of the Consumer Advisory Board of the Federal Reserve Board; she was on the Board of Governors of the New York Financial Writers Association; and she serves as a consultant to many impressive financial institutions. And she does all of this from a very impressive home office.

Surprisingly, some consultants have been able to get started with employees right from the start, even when they lacked all the capital they needed to open their doors. This bit of magic is accomplished by offering sweat equity to people who can provide help as well as money, and who might not be in immediate need of a salary or the benefits that are usually offered with conventional employment. The few instances I've heard of involved people who were working at regular jobs who invested money and part-time effort in the start-up with the goal of eventually leaving their full-time job to work for the company in which they had invested time and money.

If this appeals to you, just make sure that you never sell more than 49 percent of the stock, or the company will no longer be yours. Mel Brooks took this notion and turned it on its ear in the hilarious film, *The Producers*. The characters in this film tried to produce an intentional Broadway flop, not a success, hoping to sell far more than 100 percent of the shares of the play to unwary investors. When the show turns out to be a fantastic success, you can just imagine what happens when stockholders start looking for their rewards. If you haven't seen it, rent the DVD; it's a cautionary tale that is also hilarious.

Money is available for just about any small business, including consulting businesses, but it's harder to get for a start-up than it is for expansion and development. As you might imagine, once you have a track record, you will look a lot better to potential investors, even though your main asset—you—doesn't quite resemble the kind of asset a banker can take over and sell if things don't exactly go swimmingly.

Attracting Venture Capital

Assuming you can point to potential and a good early history, you can find money for development and expansion. A home-based consultant who has been able to build a list of satisfied clients and can show evidence of regular fee payments can usually attract venture capital from a number of sources. Again, banks are still reluctant to lend money to anyone without some physical assets that can be liquidated to repay a loan.

The money available from venture capitalists, however, usually comes with more strings attached than you might be willing to accept. Interest rates that are higher than those available from banks can be a significant problem. It's not unusual for some venture capitalists to provide money for a slice of the ownership of your company, and this is not necessarily a bad thing. However, many also take a very active interest in the start-ups in which they invest, sometimes to the point of making life difficult for the founders.

If you do seek venture capital, seek it from investors who have specialized in your type of business. They will know what you are doing and can usually be a lot more understanding than might be a venture capitalist whose primary investments are in businesses that bear no resemblance to yours. When you have to explain what you are doing every day to someone whose investments are mainly in small manufacturing companies, life can get pretty complicated.

The Service Corps of Retired Executives (SCORE) can often help by providing lists of appropriate investors. The Small Business Administration can be helpful, too. And you can more than likely find good sources through any of the associations that serve your field, or the fields of the clients you serve. Most venture capital investors look to profit mainly from the ability to sell their shares to others once your company gets on its feet.

You may have some clients who might be interested in investing in your fledgling company, but I would advise against getting money this way. This destroys the independent relationship a consultant should have and continue to maintain with his clients. If a client can provide enough work for you to survive on their billing alone, you might consider going to work for them as an internal consultant. More than a few small and large firms have people on staff who provide the services an outsider might provide. It's an enlightened company that goes this route and keeps its hands off the consulting operation. If the company is looking for someone just to front for them, this is not a good place to be. Once you've lost your integrity— whether it's as an employed internal consultant or as an independent who sells out for lavish fees—you'll "never get work in this town again" (as the saying goes).

Here is a general picture of what typical venture capitalists look for in a company in which they might invest:

- A company they feel comfortable with, that works in fields they understand
- A company that seems to be in tune with current growth areas
- The skills, education, and personal qualifications needed to make the venture work
- A market for the offered services that is not being served well by current entrenched consultants, and a market that seems to have significant expansion potential
- A company that will be of interest to those who might buy the venture capitalist's stock once the company proves itself

The amount of money venture capitalists are willing to provide varies widely from industry to industry, but as a rule of thumb they seldom go very far out on a limb with companies like consultancies, which have little or no collateral to offer.

Frequently Asked Questions

1. *What's the worst mistake you can make just starting out?*
   The worst mistake you can make is being unprepared for anything that could possibly happen that would have a negative impact on the business. Of course, this goes without saying for any and all start-up businesses. But, for a home-based consulting business, I'd have to say that not estimating the potential for start-up and growth would be the worst mistake a beginner who is doing it full-time could make. You wouldn't open a motorcycle repair shop in an area where the average age of residents is over seventy any more than you might open a consulting business where there is either no business or too much competition. For a part-timer, I'd have to say that underestimating your available time to serve your part-time clients professionally could lead to problems with your full-time job, as well as your part-time work.

2. *Is any segment of a typical economic cycle better than another to start a consulting business?*

This depends on your field and what you plan to offer. For example, as I write this we are in the second year of what is being called the worst economy since 1939. If you had been planning to start a management consulting firm specializing in high-level recruitment, it would be wiser to focus on outplacement instead. If you have broad-based human resource training and skills, you should be able to shift gears easily. It's not exactly the best time to offer office design services, but it's a good time to offer services on more economic utilization of space and site relocation.

07

Managing the Money You Make

Unless you are a financial specialist, few activities are more intimidating than the financial management of your business. Just the thought of doing your personal taxes can be daunting enough. Facing the tax issues of a business, whether it's that of a sole proprietorship or a complex corporation, can really give you the willies. Cash management is more than just putting the money in the bank and writing checks against it to pay your bills. So, most home-based consultants suggest that the first thing beginning consultants do is find and start working with an accountant right away. Just because you know how to run a set of books doesn't mean you know anything about financial management.

An accountant will not only handle the details, but he or she will provide you with the financial reality of your business. Your bank balance may show that you have a lot of money on deposit, but your accountant could tell you that you are actually losing money, and that you should consider the alternatives that are needed to either plug the leaks in your financial hull, or to power the engines of growth. The first section of this chapter will help you choose the best accountant for your consulting business.

Finding the Best Accountant for Your Business

You should have an accountant to handle your business tax work, if for no other reason. Between federal, state, and local taxes, you need someone who keeps up with the codes of each authority, and who can make sure you pay the taxes you are supposed to pay—and not a penny more. It's not a crime to pay as little tax as the law allows, but it is a crime to avoid paying taxes that you are obligated to pay.

Tax work is only the beginning, however. An accountant can also provide the financial advice you need to start your business, and to plan for the best structure it should take. It's a good idea to have an accountant go over the financial portion of your business plan. He or she can also help you register your business so that your tax liability is held to a minimum.

Most accountants can provide the bookkeeping services every home-based consulting business needs. However, it's usually better to manage part of this work yourself; there are plenty of excellent computer-based bookkeeping systems available, allowing you to save quite a bit of money. But, before you buy a computer-based program, locate an accountant and find out which of the many systems available he or she works with and which would be best for you to use. Some accountants will even give you the program you need in order to plug you into their system quickly and efficiently.

The bookkeeping and day-to-day financial elements that most often can be handled by way of a computer in conjunction with an accountant include your cash book, sales ledger, purchase records, credit and collections records, and fixed asset management records. Accountants are especially important when it comes to the preparation of financial statements, balance sheet records, profit and loss data, and cash-flow history and projections. And, if you need certain records to comply with loan applications, your accountant can prepare those, too.

In addition to handling the onerous chores related to the preparation of tax forms, accountants can be worth their weight in gold when it comes to tax planning. No one is in a better position than an accountant to help you minimize your anticipated tax obligations.

The inability to forecast cash flow accurately has sunk more than a few new, but promising consulting organizations. A good accountant should be able to help with projecting revenue streams and overall economic performance, as well as prevent you from getting into financing arrangements that may be inappropriate for a home-based business.

I recognize that not all readers are starting from scratch. If you are planning to buy an existing business, an accountant can be of immeasurable help in placing a value on the business you are thinking about buying. And, of course, when you are ready to sell your business and spend the rest of your time at the beach, an accountant can be the one who prevents you from selling too low, or pricing so high that no one makes an offer.

Choosing the Right Candidate

Start by asking for recommendations from people you know who are in similar businesses. If you don't know anyone, your banker or lawyer might be able to offer some suggestions. Make sure that the accountants you consider have experience that relates to your business and are capable of and interested in working with start-up firms.

Some accounting firms will charge by the project, some by the hour, and some use either a retainer or some form of service package. As you might imagine, if you bought an accountant's services on some sort of cafeteria arrangement, you would probably end up paying more than you might if you engaged the accountant to provide a package of services you will need regularly.

The larger the accounting firm, the less likely you will be to have any regular access to the top people in the firm. The smaller the firm, the better the access, but you will be limited to a smaller body of overall experience.

The question of whether or not your accountant should be a Certified Public Accountant (CPA) or just an accountant is an important one. Anyone can be called

Accountant Performance Rating Tips . . .

Apart from the basic qualifications, think about these factors after you have started to work with your accountant:

> Has your accountant been available when needed?

> Have reports been submitted to you on a timely basis?

> Are all charges, other than the regular charges, itemized and clearly documented?

> Has the accountant been helpful in explaining reports you do not understand?

> Has the accountant involved you in all decisions other than those which you both agree do not require consultation?

> Has the accountant informed you of tax and legislative changes that could impact your business?

an accountant, but in order to be a CPA, a person must have extensive educational credentials and then must pass very rigid tests. In order to maintain CPA status, individuals must continue to study the changing laws and meet the standards for state licensing after regular examinations.

Once you have identified several accountants who seem to be appropriate for the business you are planning, the best way to make the choice is to interview each one. If you have already done your business plan, be sure that each candidate has had an opportunity to review it. If you haven't done the plan yet and are waiting until you have an accountant to help you, be prepared with all the data you have at hand. It will be even more helpful to provide the prospective accountants with this material in advance of your meeting. Give them time to get a feel for what you are doing now and what you plan to do in the future.

Ask the individuals you meet with for their credentials as they relate to your type of consulting business. If there are others in the accounting firm, ask about others who may also work on your account. Ask about specialties, and who will be the point person on your account. You should also ask about any support staff, such as book-keepers, with whom you might interact if you give the firm your business.

Once you are comfortable with the answers to your questions about staff and professional skills, the question of charges is next. It's likely that you will either be offered a package deal, or a cafeteria type of usage of the firm's services. If you are relatively knowledgeable about accounting and finance, the cafeteria approach probably makes the most sense. But, if you are like most other start-up consultants, you will probably be better off signing on to a package program that will include all of your financial management needs. These programs lump the services of individuals in the accounting firm into one regular fee. If you go the cafeteria route, ask about how the firm differentiates its rates. You don't want to pay the same hourly rate for the firm's bookkeeping services as you do for the firm's chief tax accountant. The more routine work you can do yourself, the lower the fee will be.

Finding the Best Bank for Your Business

Too many nascent consultants turn to the banks they use for their personal accounts without doing any research at all. It's a matter of convenience, of course, but while a small savings and loan bank may know the home mortgage business inside and out, they might not have a clue about a consulting business, and especially the field in which you plan to specialize. The closer you live to large, metropolitan areas, the wider your choice of banks will be. However, unless you need regular face-to-face contact with your banker, it's possible to do your banking almost anywhere over an Internet connection.

Probably the best way to begin your search for a bank is to talk with other small business owners and get their views on the service they have experienced. That's just the first step; your next task is to determine whether your type of small business is something they understand. Years ago when I was starting my business, I talked with a banker and indicated to him that a portion of the income I received from my business would be from royalties. He told me that he knew all about this, and proceeded to talk about royalties from oil wells. He knew that I was in the publishing field, but had no idea of how royalties from books differed from oil exploration royalties. So, I talked to others on my list.

Your banker should have a variety of different business banking programs from which you can choose. A creative banker will show you how he or she can put together a banking program that addresses your specific needs if none of the bank's off-the-shelf programs provides a good-enough fit.

Be sure to ask if the bank participates in the Small Business Administration's government guaranteed loan program—and make sure that your business will qualify for participation in the program if you plan to seek finances from them.

There is hardly a bank today that doesn't have some sort of online banking program. You may want all of your clients' checks to be sent directly to your bank, but you should be notified by the bank electronically when each check clears. You don't want to send a dunning letter to a client who has sent a check to your bank which the bank has yet to clear.

Check for any special start-up programs, such as special interest rates on small business loans. Night depository is probably of no interest to you; it's mainly used by businesses such as retail stores that need to deposit their cash receipts after banking hours. But, who knows, maybe it will be important to you. Ask!

Ask about interest-bearing accounts and what the bank wants from you in return for the interest. You may want a combination checking and savings account. Ask about the credit and debit cards the bank has available for commercial accounts, and be sure to get the minimum balance levels for all the accounts the banker discusses with you.

If a bank also offers financial brokerage accounts, discuss these services, too. If you are going to park money from time to time, it probably doesn't make sense to leave it in a general bank savings account. See what they offer that provides a higher interest rate, but be sure to get all the restrictions that are placed in the investment. If you need cash in a hurry, some of these high interest rate instruments will not be for you.

As I write this, banks are merging, purging, coming, and going. It's not a stable time for banks, or for any other financial institutions, for that matter. The Federal Deposit Insurance Corporation has raised the limit on deposits it will insure, and the honchos at banks we used to revere are being called by less than flattering names. All this makes it even more difficult to select a bank for your business. I wish I had a magic formula for you to use, but I don't. You should learn as much as you can about the banks you are considering and ask a lot of questions.

Now That You Have an Accountant and a Banker . . .

Your car has a dashboard with dials, gauges, and blinking lights. Each of these signals is telling you something. A flashing red light labeled oil pressure tells you that you better pull over as quickly as possible and shut down the motor. A flashing red signal on the fuel indicator is telling you that it's time to think about finding a gas station. Both are red lights and both are warning signals, but unless you know what each is warning you about, you could either run out of gas or destroy your engine. The signals you get from your cash-reserve and cash-flow indicators could be giving you similar warnings—not about your car, but about what is going to happen to your business.

I have heard of more than a few small businesses that failed not for lack of talent on the part of the founder, or because of insufficient sales, but because the owners failed to correctly manage the money they were making. Grace Weinstein points out that the simple difference between cash in a small business and its cash flow is cause for more confusion that you might imagine. "Cash is what you have in the bank. It's not the money people owe you—it's money you have immediate access to," she says. "You may have assets that can be converted to cash, but you can't pay your bills with these assets. Cash has only one meaning, and you better keep this in mind. Profit is not cash. Profit is what you should create, but cash is what you need to run your business from day to day. Cash flow is a measure of the movement of money into and out of your business. If you have more money coming in than going out at any given time, you have a positive cash flow. If you spend more than you take in, you have a negative cash flow. In general, for a consulting business, a negative cash flow is a sign of insufficient billing, poor collection procedures, excessive operating costs, or an inability to finance unpredictable cash flow."

Managing Your Cash Flow

A well-managed business, whether it's a home-based consultancy or a global corporation, succeeds or fails in large measure by its ability to predict and manage its cash flow. Your accountant will set up a system which should allow you to see whether your regular operations will generate enough cash to meet your obligations over certain specified periods of time. Think of the reports you will get from your accountant in the same terms as the dashboard warning lights and gauges in your car. At a bare minimum, you should always have sufficient cash on hand to meet your obligations for no less than one month ahead. If the red light goes on in this area, it's time to make sure you are covered. On the other hand, if it doesn't go off, it's telling you that you may have more than enough money to meet your obligations and that you should consider doing something with the excess cash, rather than just letting it sit in the bank. You will be very much aware of what might be creating a negative cash flow, but you probably are not all that savvy about what you can do to make sure you maintain a consistently positive cash flow.

Here are a few steps you can take to increase your cash reserves and maintain a positive cash flow:

Take a More Active Role in Collecting Receivables

If you are just building a client base and a client is slow in paying, it's not easy to turn up the heat for collection. But the longer you wait to get a client on a reliable payment schedule, the more difficult it will be to collect as time goes by. Every accountant and banker will urge you to begin calls the day the payment becomes late, and to keep making them on a regular, but not-too-threatening schedule. The sooner a new client knows that he or she can't manage his or her cash flow by mismanaging yours, the better off everyone will be.

Consider Revising Your Rates

This is not easy to do, and it's a risky move, but with good reason you can either raise your rate to cover late payers or lower it to reward those who pay early. If you are surrounded by active and competent competitors, try other approaches before you consider this one.

One way to reward an early payer, or even an on-time payer, is by providing some extra service for which you don't charge, rather than altering your rate schedule. Psychologically, these random rewards are often more powerful than a significant reduction in rate. It rewards the client for good behavior, and we all remember how good it felt to get those gold stars in grade school. I have heard of a marketing consultant who adds an extra two hours of "free" consulting time for every invoice that is paid before the due date—a $600 bonus for this consultant, who bills her time at $300 per hour.

Develop New Business

Not every consultant has forty billable hours every week, so one obvious way of maintaining a positive cash flow is to increase the revenue stream from client billing. In simple terms, it just means work a little harder. As a start-up consultant, you probably know all about this. But once you get comfortable, it's tempting to slack off a bit and then wonder what happened to your cash flow and profits. I won't belabor the point—it's pretty obvious!

Reduce Your Expenses

If any of your suppliers offer cash discounts for early payment, take them; and if they don't, pay them as close to the end of the payment period as you can. If you have money in the bank that is earning interest, there's no advantage to paying any earlier than you are expected to pay. If you have any expensive equipment that can be refinanced without excessive fees or changes in interest rates, take advantage of the offers. Even if a refinance does cost a little more, gather the numbers and see what it might cost you to borrow a comparable amount of money. Go with the best deal, obviously.

Be Prepared for Short-Term Money Needs

Your banker probably explained the short-term loan arrangements his or her bank offers. Sometimes called *revolving credit loans*, these loans are arranged in advance of their need and not executed until they are needed. Most often they are based on home equity if the mortgage is held by the banker that also has your business account. In simple terms, it's a prearranged loan based on a portion of the equity available through your home mortgage, reserved just for the occasion. Don't use this source too often, though, as the rates can be high. However, if your cash-flow picture shows you a quick infusion of capital that will be gathered in the near future, it is one way to keep the ship afloat.

Keep Some Cash in Reserve

Getting back to the automobile analogy I used earlier, you should never let the tank go below a certain level. Go below a quarter tank in some parts of the country, and you may not have enough gasoline to get to the next gas station. Let your cash

Murphy on Time and Money . . .

"There is never enough time or money," and "If everything seems to be going well, you have definitely overlooked something."

reserve drop below a certain level, and you will constantly be scuttling from one place to another to keep your cash tank topped up.

Once your accountant gets an idea of how your business is going to run, he will be able to give you a figure to maintain in your bank account. You will also learn that it's a mistake to keep a lot more in that account than your accountant says you should. The money should be working for you, but it's important to invest it in instruments that are readily accessible. Buying a five-year corporate bond is not exactly good fiscal management, even if the rate is outstanding. Early redemption will probably take your interest down lower than even the lowest yield on a rural savings and loan account. Short-term certificates of deposit and Treasury Bills are favorites of most accountants when they advise on the management of cash reserve.

The Data You Need to Manage Your Company's Money

Each consulting company is unique, but most operate pretty much the same way when it comes to fiscal management. The best way to manage your money well is to have information available at all times on every major fiscal factor of your business. Your accountant will probably suggest that you operate with quarterly financial statements, which is the recommended standard. But remember: A financial statement is just a snapshot of your company's fiscal health at the time of the report. You could gain or lose a client the day after the report is issued that would alter your financial picture dramatically. Nonetheless, there are facts and figures that are relatively easy to track which will help you see trends between the issuance of quarterly reports. And, if you do use a computer to track your finances, a few regular entries of the material that is most important to you will keep you up-to-date. Remember: A computer is not just a memory bank; it's an interactive system. With a good software program, any income and expense entry will automatically adjust all the factors that are part of your accounting system, so you should be able to instantly access a screen that will tell you what you need to know.

Ask yourself the following questions about your business and see if the answers will be relevant for your view of cash flow, as well as the other figures your individual business might use:

- How much money do clients owe you that is not past due? How much money is owed you that is past due? You will need to keep tabs on these numbers to project both your short- and long-term capital needs.

- How much income are you producing on average per month, and how does this compare with your business plan projections?
- How much money do you owe for fixed expenses, such as utilities, transportation, and rent and/or mortgage payments?
- How much money do you have readily available?
- What are your monthly fixed expenses?
- Do your financial projections match those of others doing similar work?
- Does your income include steady assignments from regular clients as well as income from "walk-in" business? What is the ratio?
- Which of your services provides the most income? Of these, which provides the best net income picture (gross income less expenses)? What is the ratio of steady to random business? Beware of becoming too dependent on one client.

The answers to these questions will not only help keep you out of financial trouble, but they will also help you plan for safe growth. No matter what system your accountant uses, these are the numbers you will need, and you'll need them regularly. I have avoided giving you set-in-stone instructions simply because your accountant will have his own way of acquiring and presenting this information to you. It's like driving from New York to Washington—whether you take the direct route, the scenic route, or wander the local roads, you *will* get there. Following your accountant's map will help you to avoid the speed traps, detours, and bumpy roads.

This may seem complicated, but your accountant will probably recommend that you keep only five sets of records, from which all the data you both need can be derived. They are:

- Accounts receivable
- Accounts payable
- Payroll
- Petty cash
- Inventory

Most consultants will have no need to set up an inventory recording system. However, some will, especially those whose practice is training and human resource management. Many in this field buy inventory tests and training materials that are either charged to clients directly or are included in the overall program cost. Either way, money invested in these materials should be monitored closely.

Finding and Working with Venture Capitalists

Funding a start-up consulting business is, as I have stated several times, not easy to do. Banks aren't especially interested unless you have considerable equity in your home and are willing to pledge that equity as collateral. SBA-backed loans can make it easier. Venture capital is usually available only for young businesses whose owners can point to stable personal financial histories.

Venture capitalists are especially interested in businesses that have a potential for rapid growth. Their business is based on providing money to higher-risk businesses with rapid growth potential, with an eye toward selling the stock they get for their investment at a profit once the company has proven itself. For this risk, they can be pretty demanding in the terms they offer for the money they control. Some venture capitalists work with billions, and others with mere millions. (Remember when a million was a lot of money?)

Most venture capitalists focus on one or a few related fields. You would be unlikely to get a hearing from a venture capitalist whose field is retail fashion if you are looking for money to start a consultancy where your clients operate nuclear power plants.

Depending on your financial needs, you may discover that some venture capitalists want to provide more money than you might need, and be unwilling to make smaller investments. This may seem like rash behavior, but each venture capitalist knows pretty well how much money it takes to grow a certain business, and businesses looking for less than the minimum they are willing to invest probably don't have the rapid growth potential to make their investment profitable—or at least profitable enough for them to take the risk.

Here's the Hitch . . .

Few venture capitalists are interested in start-ups—those companies that have yet to open their doors. They are far more interested in firms that have already fledged, but have not yet grown the wings they need to soar. It's when a business first starts to show signs of good potential that they are interested, and it's usually at this point that a start-up is most often starved for capital, and when the new consultant is most vulnerable. He or she has opened the doors, brought in business, and started to build a reputation, yet is still running low on funds—unless, of course, the firm was well capitalized right from the start.

If you find yourself in this situation, try looking for short-term funds from friends, associates, and even people you may not know but who are known for making personal loans to those with good ideas and the savvy to make them work. You probably haven't met many people like this, but your accountant and your attorney probably have, and they can put you in touch with them. In a sense these people are sort of mini venture capitalists. They are doing what the full-timers do, but on a part-time basis. Over the years I have met people who do this when the right opportunity presents itself. They usually are high earners in their own profession and are looking for better and usually safer ways to invest their money than in the stock market. They don't advertise; they just let it be known to their accountant and lawyer and maybe some close associates that they could be interested if the "right deal" came along. They, like most of the larger venture capitalists, are usually looking for a significant equity position in your company.

Getting to Know Them . . .

Although there are many venture capitalists to choose from in most fields, it's usually better to see if you can get an introduction from someone who has already done business with them, or at least knows someone who has, who might be willing to provide the introduction. I don't mean to imply that a cold call won't get attention. It probably will, but when you can say that Joe So-and-So, a current client, recommended you, you will probably hear back from them a lot faster. There's nothing sneaky or sinister at all about this. The same applies to literary agents and just about any other professional service where access is often difficult to gain without an intro.

What Do Venture Capitalists Want in Return for Their Money?

The typical deal results in the venture capitalist becoming a stockholder in your corporation. (As you have probably surmised, venture capitalists and other individual investors are not all that interested in investing in partnerships or sole proprietorships.)

Depending on your ideas, what you bring to the table, and your consultancy's potential, a venture capitalist may want a substantial piece of your business. If you have a great idea, but little management ability, a venture capitalist may want to take an active part in the management of your business. He or she may even want to place someone within the firm to handle the management if you are seen as either weak in that area or too important to the implementation of the idea that attracted them in the first place. The requirements can vary a great deal.

Although most venture capitalists look to profit from their investment by selling the shares they own in your business once it becomes profitable enough, others look to a longer-term agreement and may want to be part of your business forever. And here is where you need really good advice from your lawyer and your accountant. The terms of a venture capital agreement can be very complex—far too complex for the scope of this book—so make sure your attorney and your accountant are in the loop when you think about getting money this way.

Frequently Asked Questions

1. *What is the best way to invest money in excess of that needed to maintain the business?*

   You could pay yourself an occasional bonus, but before you do, check with your accountant on the tax ramifications of such a payment. Other than that, think about the relative safety of the investments you might consider, and be sure that you are able to get your hands on the money when and if it's needed without having to pay any early sale or withdrawal penalties. Short-term certificates of deposit and simple savings accounts with decent interest rates are among the better choices. The idea is to have easy access to the money and to earn something on it—not to speculate with it!

2. *My accountant has set up my cash-flow record in three segments: operating cash, investment cash, and financing cash. Is this necessary for a small consulting business?*

   Probably not. Your accountant is probably being cautious, and might even be anticipating the time when you will be big enough to set these up as line items in your financial plan. Also, your accountant may use a program that automatically does this split, and finds it easier to follow this setup rather than to write an exception in the program.

One of the most compelling reasons people choose to work from home is the idea that tax deductions can greatly diminish the cost of operating the house they live and work in. Maybe "greatly" isn't the best word, but those deductions can make a difference, especially when you are just starting out. However, unless you know what can and cannot be included in your list of deductions, you may be invited to have a chat with the tax man.

This chapter is basically a summary of what you can and cannot do in your office and your living quarters and still expect to reduce your taxes substantially. And—please keep this in mind—tax laws change all the time. As I write this I think I can safely say that because of the current economic conditions, tax regulations will change even faster and possibly even more dramatically than they have in the past. Don't get nervous! It's my guess that most of the changes will favor you and won't add much to your tax burden.

The thrust of this chapter is to give you an overall picture of what is now possible, how you can benefit from the current laws, and what you have to do to comply. Bear in mind that whatever you do, it's critical to document everything. If you have selected an accountant and set up a computer-based financial management system, you should already have a general idea of what you can and cannot do, and how to handle everything.

Good recordkeeping is critical. You will have to record all expenses that allow you to modify your taxes, and you also want to have the kind of records that tell you whether you are in good or bad shape, and what you can do about it in either case.

I have not included any worksheets in this chapter. No two home-based consulting businesses are the same, and no two will have identical financial and tax-reporting needs. As you go through this chapter, you should be able to spot the points that will work for you. Your own checklist will become self-evident. It will then be a matter of plugging everything into the system you are using, or the one your accountant sets up, and then going after the business you need.

One more note before you dig into this chapter: Reading about taxes and paperwork can be a little depressing, so I have taken the liberty of lacing this chapter with comments from people you might recognize. I figured you might need a chuckle or two, and knowing that the rich and famous share your pain is comforting.

Taxes and Your Home Office

One of the most attractive features of working from home, other than the short commute, is that you can deduct some significant home expenses from your personal income tax. But your accountant will warn you not to go overboard. If a random audit spots an irregularity on your tax return, it's likely to result in the one thing that is worse than the dreaded blue screen of death that signals a crash on your computer—an audit! So don't put Uncle Charlie on your payroll when you know full well he still lives with Momma three thousand miles away and doesn't have a clue about a consulting business.

Can a Home Be a Tent for Tax Purposes?

I've never heard of anyone working from a tent, but according to the current tax regs, if your office has space for cooking, sleeping, and working, it could be a rented house, a house you own, a motor home, a boat, condo, co-op apartment, or maybe even a tent. I used to represent a tax consultant who also wrote books and lived with his wife on a sailboat. In summer they berthed in the Norfolk, Virginia, area, and they spent winters in southern Florida. As much as I have always liked my own home offices, this is one man I truly envied.

I should point out that the regulations can differ for a business operated outside of the house. This is a detail you will need to clear up after your accountant has a look-see.

Before you begin slashing away at your current taxes, let's take a look at the tax laws that apply to a home business:

- The space you use for your business must be used exclusively for your business. I suppose if the family dog likes to sleep in your office, the IRS would look the other way (especially if it's a pit bull).

- The office space must be in regular use; occasional use won't cut it. Your home office must be where you work regularly.
- The office must be your prime location. If you must have other locations in order to serve remote clients, they will not qualify for the tax deduction.
- If you meet with clients regularly, this must be the place where you would meet. I don't suppose you'd be nailed if you occasionally rented other sites for special meeting and occasions, but your home must serve as your main site for client and customer contact.

These are the key elements of the regulations. However, I've only given you the broad picture here; you should read the regs yourself, or ask your accountant for her take on your proposed use. For example, some local governments require that a home office have separate outside entries for clients and a separate bathroom for employees. This may have no bearing on taxes, but while you are getting the tax advice from your accountant, ask about these regs, too.

The first thing the tax folks look for is multiple use of the space. If you write client reports on a desk in the corner of your bedroom, forget about a tax deduction. Don't even think about writing off your swimming pool just because you let your clients take a dip while you work on their projects. You can probably get away with writing off some space that is used exclusively for record storage as long as you can show that you do not have sufficient storage space in the home office itself.

Direct and Indirect Expenses

Before you get carried away, don't have the house painted and expect that the IRS will look favorably on your deduction of the entire bill from your federal taxes. The IRS is very picky about how you define the space that directly relates to your business, and that which doesn't come close. And they are just as picky about how you define direct, indirect, and unrelated expenses. *Direct expenses* are those which are directly related to the business use of your home office. Painting your home office is a direct expense and can be used as a deduction, but painting the entire house and trying to convince an IRS agent that it's necessary to impress your clients won't work. Direct expenses are fully deductible, but don't get carried away. You can't deduct more than the gross income that your home office produces. The IRS wants you to be serious about your business and not just playing at it in order to claim a tax deduction.

Indirect expenses include such items as utilities, insurance, and repairs. These deductions are calculated on a proportional basis. For example, if you use 15 percent of your total home area for business, you are only permitted to deduct 15 percent of the cost of your homeowner's insurance policy. Unrelated expenses include items that you would have a tough time justifying to the IRS, such as garden maintenance. You can try, but better hope that your IRS auditor has a sense of humor. I've been told the interviews can be pretty intense.

The direct expenses are usually pretty obvious; it's the indirect expenses that get most people in trouble. Let's look at some of the indirect expenses a consultant working from a home office might be able to use for tax breaks.

Insurance

Whether you own your home or rent it, if you carry a homeowner's insurance policy on the property, you can deduct an amount equivalent to the percentage of the space you use for your home office. Most people who work from home offices usually carry additional policies which cover things their home policy might not cover. The cost of the additional policies is better treated as a direct expense for tax purposes. Shop for the best policies, even though the money you save might not be worth the time you spend comparison shopping. Just a thought!

Security

You can deduct a portion of the cost of a home security system based on your percentage of use, and there is even a depreciation allowance for your equipment.

Again, if you have a system separate from your home system, it's probably best to treat the cost as a direct expense to the business, and not as a deduction based on the cost of a system which protects the rest of your home.

Rent and Mortgage Payments

Here's where people get in the most trouble. The IRS sees rent and mortgage payments as personal expenses, and most personal expenses are not deductible. However, if you rent a home and use a portion of that home for your business office, the rental is considered an indirect expense and is deductible. If you own your home, don't even think about trying to deduct what might be the going rental rate from your taxes. The IRS doesn't smile on those who think of themselves as landlords and tenants simultaneously. It is possible, however, to claim depreciation on that part of the office in the home that you own.

Repairs

Most repairs that are necessary and have an immediate impact on the operation of your office will qualify for a tax deduction. However, you must still consider the percentage-of-use factor. For example, if your home air conditioner gives up and your office is cooled by this system, the amount you can claim will still be based on the percentage of the total space the office occupies. If your office has a window air conditioner that has no effect on the rest of the house, that repair will be deductible. If any significant repairs are needed, you will probably have to depreciate the cost, so check with your accountant before you spend the money.

Property Taxes

If local regulations permit you to have a home office, you can deduct the appropriate percentage from your taxes.

Moving Costs

If local regulations permit a home office, the appropriate portion of the cost of a move can be deducted.

Other Tax Deductions

While it would be a mistake to not take advantage of some of the other tax deductions that are available, it would be an even bigger mistake to try to take advantage of every tax break. You'd never get any work done. Just remember that everything you claim must be documented with careful and detailed records.

Your accountant will be able to give you the advice you need on which tax breaks are worthwhile and which ones are not. Her list will be based specifically on your particular business. For example, if you use Internet services for both business and personal reasons, you can only deduct the time you spend online doing business as a business expense. If your online business time is extensive, your accountant might suggest that you record it and pro-rate it for tax purposes. For anyone else, that kind of minutiae would be mind-numbing and counterproductive. So, with this in mind, here's a list for you to chew on. I've done it in Q&A format to make it easier and more relevant to individual reader interests.

Q. One of my clients closed down without paying me for two completed projects. Can this be deducted as a bad debt?

A. If you operate on a cash basis, as most home-based businesses do, you can't do this. If you had loaned the client some money, the debt would be deductible. On the other hand, if you operate on an accrual basis and had already reported the debt as income, it would not qualify. There has to be an actual loss of money to qualify.

Q. My one computer is used for home as well as business. Can I deduct any of the cost for business use?

A. If you can clearly document the business-related use, you can deduct the business portion of the cost. There are two ways you can do this, and it's best to get advice from your accountant regarding which would be of more benefit to you for your particular business. Your accountant should be able to explain the hobby-loss regulation in fewer words than it would take here. And, besides, we're probably talking about peanuts anyway.

Q. Are sales taxes on products and supplies I buy for my business deductible?

A. You can deduct sales taxes on supplies, but you can't deduct sales taxes on capital assets you purchase. Your accountant will tell you how to capitalize the sales tax on the cost of any taxable assets you purchase.

Q. What is the difference between a business expense and a business asset?

A. For tax purposes, a business asset is something of value you acquire which you plan to use in your business for more than one year. Tangible things such as computers and intangible things such as patents are, then, assets.

A business expense is money spent on products and some services to be used in the current tax year. For tax purposes, business expenses can be deducted immediately from income. You will have to spread out the cost of an asset, and it must be deducted over more than a year. Don't guess here; if you are in doubt about how to classify something, ask your accountant. You could find yourself three or four years later having to explain your reasoning to the IRS, and possibly paying back taxes as well as some interest and penalties.

Q. What about business-travel expenses?

A. If the main purpose of the trip is business-related, there is a lot you can deduct from your taxes. For example, you can deduct train fare and airfare, hotel room charges, and even some of the incidentals such as laundry, cab fare, car rental, and phone calls. You can only deduct half of your meal costs and your costs to entertain a client. There's a lot more, so play it safe and ask your accountant for her advice on the current items that are currently deductible.

Q. Suppose I plan to visit some clients while on vacation with my family; what portion of those expenses are deductible?

A. The best advice I can give you, given the space available in this book, is to check with your accountant. While many of the expenses are deductible, it gets complex, so you should check with your accountant to be sure. Be sure to document everything and keep all records and receipts.

Storing and Retention of Records

What You Can Store on the Computer

If you use an accountant and that accountant uses a data-based accounting system—who doesn't these days?—most of the critical financial records and numbers will be filed on the program database. Since computers have been known to eat data from time to time, it makes sense to count on more than the memory in your hard drive for these records. Probably the best way to protect yourself is to burn discs of all your critical material and to keep these discs somewhere other than the location of your computer, or probably even away from the home office itself. There are online data storage services available that are probably quite safe. However, I have always been inclined to go the do-it-yourself route with discs I burn and store about a mile from my home office.

The disc route can get clunky, and you might want to think about a portable hard drive on which you can store your material. The advantage here is that you can overwrite material more quickly when you go to update information than you can when you use the CD-RW disc approach. However, a portable hard drive can get some pretty rough treatment; while the data may not be disturbed if yours gets dropped, you may never be able to access it because of mechanical failure. The little driveless memory sticks are ideal for transferring data and for short-term storage, although there seems to be some debate about how long the data can remain viable. CDs seem to be far more durable, and they are so inexpensive that in my opinion, this seems to be the way to go.

What to Do With All the Stuff You Can't Put on Your Computer

It would be nice if you could save all your records electronically; all you'd probably need would be a few discs that would take up no space at all. Unfortunately, there will be a lot of data coming your way that must be saved and cannot be put on a computer easily.

I suppose you could scan all the manuals that come with your equipment and save them as PDF files. You could even scan all of your receipts, legal documents, utility bills, and so on, but you wouldn't have much time left to do the things that make money. So, as onerous as it may seem, you still have to set up a system for storing these and many other documents that you will acquire as the owner of a home-based business. A hybrid system using both your computer and some file cabinets has to be somewhere in your plans.

Whether it gets saved to a disc or filed in a drawer will be up to you, and the decision will probably be determined by the way the data arrives to you. What you receive online will be saved electronically. What arrives in an envelope will probably be saved in a filing cabinet. So much for this blinding glimpse of the obvious!

Since I can't lay claim to being the most organized person in the world, I turned to an expert, Roberta Roesch, who has written many articles and books on the subject. As a result of our conversations, I have at least started to organize the data that can't be easily saved electronically in a better way.

I asked Roberta how someone who might be accustomed to working for a large firm that is already well organized should face the task of setting up a home office filing system. Her reply: "It's critical for someone running a small home business to have a calendar specifically devoted to the things that will occur regularly and predictably. Leave space to include events that have to be marked as you go along, but the basic calendar should include such items as pay schedules, tax payment dates, equipment maintenance schedules—anything and everything that has a date critical to the running of your business should be on it."

Even well-planned and carefully documented calendars aren't perfect, and Roberta has a suggestion for that. "If you keep a paper calendar, get a set of different-colored magic markers and devote a color to each different event. Highlight taxes in red," she says with a wry smile. "If you keep your calendar electronically, simply use the range of colors available on your word processing program." For those who really like to play it safe, she suggests using both an electronic-based calendar and a paper calendar. "After you get it set up with all the different recurring dates and color coding, just print it out and use both." She acknowledges that this has its problems. "If you keep two records of the same events, you must be sure that each jibes with the other. It's added work, but not too much work if safety is the issue for you," she said.

A calendar is just the beginning; equally as important is the system you use to file the paperwork you need to save. Roberta advises that you file alphabetically by category, or by date, and continues, "I'd suggest that consultants who work from a home office are probably better off if they file chronologically by category. However, this is a very subjective area; it's probably best to start this way and then shift to another arrangement if the system doesn't seem to be what you need."

Roberta explains that a system based on the frequency of use makes a lot of sense for the typical consulting operation. "Setting up a file for items that must be retained for long period of time, but is referred to infrequently, is a good way to deal with such things as insurance policies, rental and lease agreements, bank records, and license and permit renewals. Another file for more frequently used files, such as correspondence, payroll records, supplier records, and invoice and payment records makes good sense."

All of this, of course, begs the question: How long should records be kept? Given that many of your records can be kept electronically, I'd suggest that you keep everything forever. After all, you never know when you might need some data, regardless

Filing System Tip . . .

A filing system should work for you—you shouldn't be a slave to it. The whole idea is to make it easier for you to do the work for which you get paid. The more complex you make it, the less likely you are to lose something or miss an important date. But the more time you spend filing, the less time you will have for doing productive, billable work. You will change and shift things as you go along until you reach a point where your recordkeeping system is perfect for you and the work you do. Organization expert Roberta Roesch suggests: "Even though you may have arrived at a system which you are comfortable with, take the time occasionally to think about how you might make it better. In this case, you will find that better is defined as no loss of precision, but a gain of time by eliminating some redundancy."

of whether it is mandatory to retain the records. For example, if you were doing some long-range financial planning and you wanted some of your financial data that is past the expiration date set by the Fed, you'd be out of luck if you erased it. If you are keeping your records on paper, stick to the regulation dates as a minimum, but if you have the space to spare, hang on to them until you are absolutely sure that you will never need them again.

Record Retention

Here are some general guidelines for record retention:

- Keep your canceled checks, receipts, and all other documents that might be needed to document a claim for at least as long as the statute of limitation requires for each item. Your accountant can fill you in on these dates.
- You should keep all documentation of your federal tax returns for three years from the date the tax return was filed, or two years from the date the tax was actually paid, whichever is longer.
- Some records should be kept forever, or at least until they are no longer valid. These include most of your corporate records, property records, and all insurance documents. If you employ others in the operation of your business, you are currently required to hang on to all employment tax records for at least four years.
- For all other records, and there will be plenty of them, the decision should be made based on what the law requires and what would be the most difficult to replace if you needed them and couldn't lay your hands on them.

Until fairly recently, most decisions to save or chuck were made when you began tripping over the storage boxes on the way to your desk. Now that it is possible to store most of your sensitive data on a simple compact disc, it just makes sense to do what you can that way and never to chuck anything. Whether you put one or five gigabytes of data on a disc is immaterial. The physical size of the disc is the same. And, if you are like some others, including me, I have a dupe of every disc stored at a different location.

A Parting Shot

Ask the average home businessperson—whether a consultant, a manufacturer's rep, or a freelance writer—what bugs them most about their business, and they will all tell you the same thing: paperwork. Managing paperwork is the subject of hundreds of books. Books on accounting recordkeeping are done as a series, and could very well by sold by the yard or by the pound. So, if I failed to include something that is close to your heart, forgive me. Before I leave the subject and move on to another—law, which has more written about it than recordkeeping—here's what some people you might recognize have said about (ugh) paperwork.

Julia Louis-Dreyfus
She, of the now-syndicated and still-popular TV show, *Seinfeld*, said, "I've actually considered going with my married name, Julia Hall, but all the paperwork . . ."

Frank Zappa
Guitarist, composer, film director, you name it, Zappa said, "It isn't necessary to imagine the world ending in fire or ice. There are two other possibilities: one is paperwork and the other is nostalgia."

Pearl Bailey
The multitalented Bailey nailed it with this statement: "The sweetest joy, the wildest woe is love. What the world needs is more love and less paperwork."

Wernher von Braun
One wonders whether we might have gotten to the moon sooner from Dr. von Braun's comment: "We can lick gravity, but sometimes the paperwork is overwhelming."

C. Northcote Parkinson
You have met this insightful man in earlier chapters, and here he continues to be as witty and relevant as you might expect: "The man whose life is devoted to paperwork has lost the initiative. He is dealing with things that are brought to his notice, having ceased to notice things for himself."

Peter De Vries
He, too, sees paperwork as anathema: "I love being a writer. I just can't stand the paperwork."

Frequently Asked Questions

1. *What effect do the home office deductions have on the taxes that must be paid when the house with a home office is sold?*

   In some cases, taxes will be levied that could reduce the real value of the deductions taken. However, you may be willing to put up with this, especially when every nickel counts in the start-up phase. This is a complex issue and not easily answered in a few sentences. Just make a note somewhere to check with your accountant when you plan to sell your house. Some accountants claim that, based on the deductions taken and the downstream consequences, it could be better to forgo some of the deductions that are available to you. Get a professional opinion before you do anything!

2. *What are the chances that I will face a federal audit?*

   Actually, they are pretty remote, unless you begin earning a lot of money rather quickly. The IRS has a number of red-flag issues that will trigger an audit, but it usually takes one dramatic event, or a combination of different red-flag events, before the alarm is sounded. In general, the more you make, the more likely you are to be audited. Most other audits are done randomly.

3. *Is there anything available from the IRS to help me get started?*

   The IRS has a number of very helpful reports and guides, available at www.irs.gov/businesses/small.

Is It Legal?

No matter how big or small your business, regardless of whether you work from your home or an office building you own, almost everything you do to run a business will be governed by laws. These laws are designed to protect you as well as your clients. You can complain all you want about this or that law restricting you in one way or another, but I'm sure you will be glad when a law you never heard of comes to your rescue—for example, when a client refuses to pay your fee.

Not only will you have to conform to local, state, and federal laws about the formal conduct of your business, but you will also have to conform to laws enacted by your community and state that govern what you can and cannot do in and with your home office. Again, these laws protect you as well as restrict you, so grin and bear it if you find some of them to be a burden. If you find anything especially troublesome, there's nothing to stop you from either seeking a waiver or even seeking to have a particular law changed.

This chapter is divided in two parts. The first part deals with the laws involved in setting up your business. The second part focuses on the laws that protect you, along with the laws that protect others from you (if you happen to break a particular law).

Law and a Home Business Start-Up

There is no law that says you need an attorney to start your business, and it's not all that complicated to get the right forms, fill them out accurately, file them, and open your doors. However, I believe it's a big mistake to take this step without the aid of an attorney.

If your business is subject to the regulations of any local, state, or federal laws, you should get advice from an attorney on your specific needs and plans.

If your consulting work requires any special personal or licensing requirements, you could read the laws on the books. However, you'd never know how those laws may have been interpreted by others who may have run afoul of them in the past. If your small and friendly town has enacted laws that prevent you from running certain types of businesses from a home, you need legal advice. In short, obtaining sound legal advice, however costly, is money well spent.

What follows in this chapter is *not* legal advice. However, it is advice that has been gathered from many people who have started and run small businesses, and from lawyers who have helped them do it. Think of what follows as a basic guideline to get you started.

There are four basic ways to structure your business, each with different requirements that define the benefits to you and your responsibilities as the owner of the business. Each differs in its complexity and its ability to protect you, if you should ever need protection.

The Sole Proprietorship

The sole proprietorship is the easiest form of ownership to set up and manage. You make all the decisions. You don't have to consult with others if you want to expand the business, take money out of it, or even seek financing. There's nothing to prevent you from using your personal checkbook for all business transactions, and you can even offset business losses on your personal tax return. It costs less than the others to start up, there are far fewer regulations that you must stick with, and there is a lot less paperwork to deal with.

Sounds like the perfect way to go, doesn't it? It is, unless you consider that the big string attached to this form of ownership is that you are also personally liable for all debts and legal actions brought against you as a result of your business activities. It's usually a lot more difficult to get financing to start a sole proprietorship, and getting operating capital can be a problem unless you are willing to put your home up for collateral. Even then, all you can get is the amount you presently own based on your down payment and the amount you have paid off so far.

When you die, the business comes to an end, too. You can make arrangements in advance for someone to take it over if anyone is interested, but it's usually difficult to find people who are willing to work for a sole proprietorship. The rules governing the fringe benefits you can take for yourself, such as pension plans and health insurance, can be quite limiting.

Having said this, if you don't plan to build a big firm and can live with the limitations, it's not a bad way to operate. You may be able to get better protection as a corporation, but even then you are not totally risk-free. The issue of risk protection is best discussed with your attorney, who can explain how you can, as a stockholder of the corporation, be held liable for suits based on the number of shares you own.

The Partnership

Two or more people make a partnership. In many ways a partnership is like a sole proprietorship, except that there is more than one person in the organization. The management and operation of a partnership is based on the mutual agreement of the partners. A partnership must have at least one general partner (but can have more than one); this person is authorized to act for the others in such activities as signing agreements that obligate the partnership; hiring employees; and making purchases for the firm. There are a number of different types of partnerships, and your attorney can explain the advantages and disadvantages of each as they relate to your personal requirements.

One of the major benefits of a partnership is the freedom it offers partners to take money out of the firm. This is one of the reasons why so many law firms are set up as partnerships. A partnership makes it easier to pool investments in the business than is possible in a corporation. Partnerships can be set up quickly and easily to accomplish specific goals, and when the work has been completed, they can be just as easily dissolved. It's not as easy to shut down a corporation. Depending on the state and local area in which a partnership is set up, there are usually fewer regulations you need to adhere to, and lower operating costs to consider.

Partnerships are not liable for income taxes. The profits and losses are the tax liabilities of the individual partners. This, of course, means that the tax carry-forward benefits of a corporation are not available to partners.

> **Partnership Tip . . .**
>
> Depending on the state in which you live, your spouse may have a legal interest in your partnership, regardless of whether or not he or she takes an active role in the business. Given that half the marriages in the U.S. seem to end in divorce, you may have to buy out a divorced spouse. Check with your lawyer if this applies to you.

The major problem with partnerships is the liability each partner has for the actions of the other partners. If a partner makes a commitment and skips town, the other partners can be held liable for any commitments the wicked partner may have made.

Although it isn't required, you and any partners you are planning to have should have a written agreement in which all the partners' rights and responsibilities are spelled out clearly. This is a job for an attorney; don't try to do it yourself. There's a lot to consider before you meet with your attorney. He or she will probably give you a list of questions to answer before the meeting, and might even give you a copy of the Uniform Partnership Act. This act has been adopted by all states, except for Louisiana. Some states have made amendments to the code which are applicable only in their state. However, the spirit of the code and much of the detail is the same from state to state.

Here are the points you should be prepared to discuss with your attorney when you and your partners meet to prepare your partnership agreement. Remember, most attorneys charge by the hour, so do your homework in advance.

- The purpose and function of the partnership (try to be more detailed than just saying you plan to run a consultancy)
- The name of the firm (be careful about using all the partners' names; if anyone leaves the firm, it will be necessary to rename it, and that will be a legal expense)
- The life of the partnership, if it is to have a finite life
- The responsibilities and authority of each partner
- The number and type of partners; partners can be silent, general, limited, and just about anything you want to have, as long as your definition is in sync with the Uniform Partnership Act
- A definition about how profits and losses will be apportioned
- The requirements for the admission of new partners
- A plan for dissolving the partnership
- A description of what each partner will bring to the table, which should include work to be done, money to be contributed, equipment, contact lists, and just about anything else that would benefit the partnership
- A detailed plan of how the financial and other records will be kept
- Agreed-upon methods of dispute resolution between partners

- A plan for portioning property bought in the name of the partnership
- A partner buyout plan
- A plan to handle partner disabilities

This is just a general outline. Use it as a beginning for your discussions and try to have all the answers in hand before you meet with your attorney.

Most partnerships begin with capital supplied by the working partners. However, there are times when the firm may need more money than any of the partners have or may be able to borrow. When this is the case, a limited partnership is usually established, which includes people whose only contribution to the partnership is capital. Limited partners are only held liable for the amount of money they bring to the partnership, not for the debts or actions of the other partners.

The Corporation

Under law, a corporation is thought of in the same terms as a person. That is, the corporation can enter into contracts, own property, lend and borrow money, plus do many other things. The main feature for those who go the corporation route is usually the ability take advantage of tax laws unavailable to other forms of business; the ability to attract investors; and a certain amount of personal legal protection that is unavailable to the other organizational structures.

Size doesn't matter, and in many cases it isn't worth it for a very small business to incorporate. Your lawyer can give you the advice you need when she knows the full picture of the company you envision. In the meantime, here are some of the benefits of the corporate form of organization:

- It can be easier to raise start-up capital as a corporation. You can sell stock privately, and may not have to seek money from banks and other commercial sources. Keep in mind, however, that whether or not you are incorporated, banks and other lending institutions take the same view of your ability to repay as will most other sources.
- Your tax rate may be lower, but this may come at a price. Your accountant can tell you why when he or she has the complete picture.
- It's generally easier to transfer ownership in a corporation than it is with other forms of organization. You can sell your corporate stock, but you have nothing to sell as a partnership. A partnership must be dissolved and reestablished if it is to pass to others.

- You can set up more fringe benefits for yourself under a corporate structure than you might be able to under any of the other forms.
- If you have employees and any of them causes the corporation to be sued, you are better insulated from the suit than you might be under any other form.
- If growth beyond a one-person consultancy is in your plan, it's easier to attract good employees to a company structured as a corporation than any other form. Stock ownership is a tempting carrot for many people.
- There are many estate planning benefits available that are not available to other forms.
- If there is even the slightest hint that your partners might be contentious, the corporation is the best way to go. A parting of the ways doesn't involve dissolution of a corporation as it does with a partnership.

As attractive as the corporate structure can be, there are a few downside issues that must be considered. The main problems are:

- There is far more paperwork required to operate a corporation than any of the other forms. The records that you are legally obliged to keep can wear you down very quickly.
- It does cost more to operate as a corporation than it does to operate any of the other forms. Accounting fees are higher, mainly because of the amount of documentation the various taxing authorities require. The legal fees to incorporate will be higher, too.
- A corporation is required to pay taxes on its profits before it distributes dividends to stockholders who must also pay taxes on the money they receive. It's not exactly double taxation, but the amounts can eat into what you thought should be yours. There are legal ways to make sure that this isn't a big problem, but the legal and accounting advice needed to help you maximize your personal income will be costly. If you think that bumping up your salary might eliminate the profits on which your corporation might have to pay taxes, forget about it. The IRS is permitted to set salary levels and dividends if it sees evidence of this ploy.
- As a sole proprietor you can run your business from your personal checkbook. But as a corporation, if you make a payment on a personally owned car from your corporate checkbook, you will be in trouble.

What I have just described is a typical "C" corporation. There are two variants of the corporate structure that can often be more appealing and more practical to those starting small, home-based consulting businesses. They are the "S" corporation and the limited liability corporation (LLC). In case you've noticed the letters LLC along with MD and DDS, and thought they represented some sort of therapeutic achievement, they don't. They simply announce that these businesses have been set up as limited liability corporations, a corporate structure that has been deemed appropriate for the individuals or small groups involved.

An "S" corporation offers many of the taxation benefits of a partnership, and limited liability protection from creditors. The income, deductions, and tax credits of an "S" corporation must go to the shareholders annually, even if distributions are not made. This limits your ability to balance good years with bad years as you can under the "C" corporation tax regulations.

Those who own an LLC are called members, not stockholders, and are treated differently for both tax and liability purposes. Members can elect to be taxed as sole proprietors, partners, or as "S" or "C" corporations. Many states, however, levy a franchise tax on these forms of corporations. There is less paperwork to deal with, and the problem of double taxation is eliminated unless the members elect to be taxed as a "C" corporation. In most states the LLC can be established with just one member, and memberships can be assigned to others without having to restructure the corporation.

Because of the variety of possibilities in these two forms of organizations, it's best to talk with your attorney and accountant and let them help you decide which form would be best for the organization you envision.

Law and the CYA Factor

You may never need the services of a lawyer again after you set up your business. But, then again, you may. Suppose a client is unhappy with what you have done for him. You know your work meets professional standards. You know what you are doing, and you have consulted on similar projects for years without ever encountering an unhappy client. In short, suppose that you have run up against one of those people whose sole reason for being seems to be to get something for nothing—including your professional services.

How can someone sue you under those circumstances? Any number of ways, actually; for example, think about the negligent misrepresentation ploy. The client claims that you misrepresented your credentials in a way that diminishes your ability to provide the services you claim to be able to provide. It's almost impossible to make a case for something like this, but your client's lawyer has filed a suit, and it has been accepted by the court. You have been paid half of your fee, and you have submitted your report and billed the client for the balance of the fee. But the client is making claims that because of your recommendations, he lost money on a deal, and he is now suing to recover that money. There could be a lot of money at stake, but you get the sense that if you agree to return the fee paid so far, and agree to void the second invoice, all will be forgiven. The money involved is a lot more than your fee, so it seems prudent to call it quits and find better clients. But, is it? If you had established a connection with an attorney, you would quickly be shown just what was happening, and for a few bucks you would probably get your entire fee mandated by the court.

It's not often that a consultant will need a lawyer, but it's a lot better to have an established contact than it is trying to find a lawyer in the Yellow Pages at the last minute, when you've been handed a summons to appear in court. Here are just a few of the situations you might encounter where legal assistance is needed:

- Whenever you sign an agreement that involves a significant amount of money
- Whenever you sign an agreement that commits you to a long and time-consuming project
- Whenever you sign an agreement that is difficult to understand
- When you agree to take on an employee who might become your competitor at some point in the future
- When you have intellectual property that you need to protect
- Whenever you alter the form of your business or start another business

These are just a few of the more common situations which usually require the professional assistance of an attorney. Your needs will be different from those of any other consultant, so there is probably little you can turn to in the library or even on the Internet to help you out. But if you have selected your attorney carefully, he or she should know enough about your business to help quickly and without having to do the research that an attorney you picked from the Yellow Pages might have to do.

Finding a Lawyer

The best way to find an attorney who will be most able to help you is to seek refer-rals from others who are working in the same field as you. If you strike out, check the listings of any professional or trade associations you belong to. Many maintain listings as well as comments from members on how helpful they might have been in specific situations. If your local library has a copy of the Martindale-Hubbell Law Directory, that's also a good place to start (or you can check out www.martindale .com). The one thing you want to avoid is talking to your uncle's wife's third cousin who is a lawyer—unless, of course, he or she happens to specialize in your field. Just because you may be related to a divorce lawyer is not a good enough reason to make the choice if, indeed, the lawyer agrees to work with you.

Here are some general guidelines to help you in your search:

- Ask if there is a charge for the first meeting, or initial consultation. Some lawyers will meet with you briefly to make sure neither of you would make a mistake by establishing a relationship. If you get to the point of an initial consultation, it's fair for the attorney to charge you for the time spent.
- Ask the attorney for details about his or her experience handling work similar to the work you will need done. Most lawyers can tell you in general terms what they have done, and for whom, without revealing any confiden-tial details. (If an attorney seems to be hedging on details, it's probably not because he has nothing to say, but because he may have too much to say that he cannot divulge.)
- If it isn't already apparent, ask about the type of clients the attorney repre-sents. If none are familiar, ask how his or her experience with these clients relates to the issues on which you might need counsel.
- Try to see where you will stand in terms of the size and importance of the other clients the attorney works with. You want to make sure that even though you may be small relative to his or her other clients, that you will still get the service you need when you need it. If the lawyer you choose is recognized as a specialist in your field, all the better; however, remember that specialists can be costly.
- Legal fees can be high, so make sure you know what fees will be involved. You may be charged by the hour, or the attorney may be willing to work for a percentage of any settlement in your favor. Make sure you and the attorney

see eye to eye on the money before any counseling is begun. If others on the staff, such as researchers, are to be involved, ask how their services will be billed.

- If you are working with a large firm, make sure that you meet with and approve of the staff attorney who will handle your case. Don't hesitate to ask if there might be another attorney to consider if you are uncomfortable with the person the firm might assign to your case.
- Ask about the kind of backup the staff has. If research is involved, you need to know that those doing it understand the elements of your case.

What Will It Cost?

Most often legal services are billed by the hour. I wish I could give you a range of fees, but there are so many variables involved that such numbers would be very misleading. If you are working with the big specialist in your field, your fee will be much higher than it might be if you were working with someone else. Where you and your lawyer are located can make a difference, too. A lawyer in New York City is likely to charge more than a lawyer in a small and remote suburb. Wherever you are, get an estimate of the total costs and how much time will be involved. Keep in mind that you and your lawyer may be able to put a case together quickly, but it could be quite a while before it even gets to trial.

If the lawyer works on a retainer basis, you will be asked to pay an amount up front. The money will be held in an account from which the lawyer draws his or her fee as the work progresses. If your case involves the possibility of a large cash settlement if you prevail in court, the lawyer may be willing to work for a percentage of the settlement. Such arrangements are seldom based on less than 25 percent of the settlement.

There can be a lot of loose ends here, so be sure to get everything in writing, and make sure you understand just what the attorney is expected to do for you.

Keeping Legal Fees Down

Chances are that any suits you face might be best handled by an attorney on an hourly basis. The best way to keep these costs down is to know what you are talking about whenever you and your attorney meet. Be sure you are familiar with all the issues of the case, and do some reading on what others might have done in similar situations.

You probably can get good information from any groups or associations you belong to where other members might have had a similar legal experience. As a writer, I belong to two organizations: the Authors Guild and the American Society of Journalists and Authors. Both do an excellent job of reporting and commenting on legal issues. Given the number of professional and trade associations in the country, I'm sure that your field is covered by at least one of them. If your meetings with your lawyer can focus on the merits and potentials of the case, rather than each of you briefing the other, you can save quite a bit of money.

The word *standard* doesn't mean that each party must agree to each and every point. Boilerplate contracts are jumping-off points from which individual variations can be made as long as both parties agree. For example, every book publisher has a boilerplate agreement which is based on the publisher's experience over its years in business. Many of these terms are negotiable. The advance money amount is almost always negotiable, and it doesn't require a lawyer to make it legal. Most literary agents are not lawyers, but it's one of their major responsibilities to their authors to negotiate the terms of a publisher's contract offer.

If your attorney is charging you an hourly rate, the clock ticks whether you are meeting face-to-face, or by telephone, or probably by any of the recent electronic communication systems, such as Skype. Do your research, plan the conversation carefully in advance, and you will not only be able to keep your costs down, but you will probably be a lot more helpful to your attorney.

Typical Legal Issues

Do You Need a Contract with Every Client?

If you are talking about work that might be considered substantial in your field, you should have a contract. Oral agreement can be enforced if there is sufficient documentation, but the recoverable amounts are usually pretty small. However, most consulting agreements, even for smaller, home-based consultants, can run into many thousands of dollars. When this kind of money is in play, both you and your client should sign off on something, and the contract that has become the "standard" in your field is the best place to begin.

You can also prepare a letter of agreement, which will have about the same legal force as a formal contract, as long as you both agree to it, sign off on it, and have your signatures notarized. Only you and your client can make the decision, but if you stick to the notion that the agreement keeps both of you from making mistakes or heading in the wrong direction, it's the best way to go.

The courts will accept a letter of agreement that has not been prepared by an attorney, but in most cases these are the tests that must be passed for its acceptance:

- The letter of agreement should be worded in such a way that one party offers to do something for another party in return for some specific compensation—in most cases, money.
- The letter should include the terms of acceptance of the work to be performed.
- There must be a clear description of what you offer to do.
- A completion date should be specified.
- The amount of the payments, how the payments are to be made, and any schedule of payments should be included.
- Both parties should agree on a method to resolve problems that might arise if either party fails to live up to the agreement. This could include whether to resolve the dispute by way of a court of law or by arbitration. It should also describe how attorney, arbitrator, and court costs should be assigned.

Every field has its list of potential legal issues. Consultants don't seem to be overburdened by litigious issues, but here are a few you should be aware of:

- An employee who leaves and competes directly with you: Every state seems to have a different take on this issue. In most cases there are some measures that can be taken, but most of them address limited geographic areas where someone might compete, or the time for which someone might be prevented from competing with you. If this could be a problem, ask your attorney about the laws in your state, and have her draft an agreement for the person to sign.

- A client can sue you if he or she feels that you failed to deliver what you promised. This is usually tough to prove, but it can be costly to defend in court. Your best defense is writing a very clear statement about what you are expected to do and making it part of any other agreement you may make with clients regarding the work you will do for them.

- You can sue a client, too. The decision to go to court should be made on the basis of real damages, not just to get even. If you can do it in small claims court, you won't need to be represented by an attorney. But if the amounts are above the limits set by the courts in your state, your decision to sue someone rests pretty much on the damages you claim to have suffered at the hands of the client, how much it might be possible to collect as a result of these damages, and what it will cost to bring a successful suit.

Frequently Asked Questions

1. *What are the major drawbacks of the corporate structure for a solo practitioner?*

   There is much more paperwork involved than there would be for a sole proprietorship. Accounting fees are higher than they might be for a corporation, and a corporation has to pay corporate taxes. Unless you are operating in a notoriously litigious environment, you are probably better off not incorporating. Any personal protection the corporation offers can be breached if a claim brought against you is valid.

2. *Is it safe to work from a home office without first checking for local regulations?*

   It's not a good move. Check local ordinances first. You will probably find that unless you expect a parade of people to come and go to your home office, no one will care. If there are ordinances which might hinder you, it's usually possible to get a variance if those people the town is trying to "protect" give their assent. You certainly don't want to establish and run a business for a few years and suddenly find the sheriff at your door with a big padlock.

3. *Should I draw up a contract for every consulting assignment I take on?*

   A formal contract may not be necessary, but whatever you do for a client, you should have something in writing that states your rights and responsibilities as well as those of your client. Such a letter of agreement, signed by you and your client, will allow both of you to relax and do what you agreed to do in the first place.

10 Creating Your Marketing Plan

Your marketing plan, like your business plan, is a tool. It should be used to build your business in an orderly way. It should keep you focused on certain attainable goals, and it should be flexible enough to help you navigate unanticipated roadblocks, as well as to take advantage of positive conditions you didn't foresee when you wrote it.

A good marketing plan is based on a clear understanding of who and what your target market is. Your target market is made up of potential clients for the specific service or services you plan to offer. To be most effective, your marketing plan should provide you with clear answers to these four critical questions:

- What services are needed, and how are you able to provide them?
- Is there a large-enough market for your services so that you can serve the potential clients economically from your geographic area?
- Are your potential clients in a position to pay the fees you will need to charge in order to prosper?
- How will you promote your services efficiently and economically?

As mentioned in my discussion of business plans in chapter 4, your marketing plan can be either elaborate and complex, or simple and uncluttered. It really depends on how much detail you feel you need. What follows will help you create a basic marketing plan that can launch your business with a minimum of fuss, and it can also be used as the basis of a far more elaborate plan if that's what you want. It's way beyond the scope of this book to describe a complex plan in one chapter, but there are many good sources and templates you can use if you choose to write a complex plan.

Answer These Questions First

Since the Q&A format tends to reduce things to basics, I have taken that approach to guide you in creating your marketing plan. Not all questions require elaborate answers, but all of them should be answered. Some may be more relevant to the service you plan to offer, and others may be only tangentially relevant. Whatever the case may be, don't ignore any of them. Take your time and answer each question thoughtfully. Strive for clarity, not style. If one word will do, fine! If it takes pages to answer some questions, so be it.

What do you want your marketing plan to do for the services you plan to offer?
In the simplest terms you can use, write a few paragraphs on what you hope to gain from marketing your services. Produce immediate income? Enhance income you may already have from some consulting work? Introduce new services? Tap different markets? I think you can see where I'm going with this. Don't get lofty and grandiose—just keep it simple and direct. Call it your marketing mission statement if that helps you see it more clearly

What consulting services will you offer, what do you expect your income to be from these services, and what strategic goals do you have?
Now it's time to get down to brass tacks. Describe the consulting services you plan to offer in some detail. For example, it won't be enough to simply state that you plan to consult with automotive aftermarket parts distributors. Will you be consulting on sales? Stocking and warehousing? With which level of your client company will you interact? Will you be implementing any of the results of your consulting? This kind of detail is important, so take the time you need to be specific. You should have some target numbers as a result of the financial planning I discussed in chapter 7; include them here.

How do you envision the following elements of your proposed company?

- *The company culture.* Every organization, even if it's made up of just one person, has a company culture. It's the way you would like your prospects and clients to see you. It's the image you feel that would best position you to achieve your goals.
- *The strengths of your company.* Since you are probably a one-person organization at this point, think about what you can bring to the table that a client needs, and that prospects will feel might be important in order to offer

you an assignment. It's important to note that while some of your strengths may not be what you want to focus on, you should list them anyway. Until you get to know a client, you won't know what rules his or her decision-making process; the more you can offer, the better your chances of getting the business you want.

■ *The weaknesses of your company.* Be honest! If you are doing qualitative market research and you have no feel for the quantitative side, make a note of it. You might want to rank-order them so that you can see where improvement might be made more easily and where you should avoid pitching business.

How do you see your potential customer base?

You should have a pretty good idea of how much typical potential clients spend on the services that you plan to offer in your marketing area. Now is the time to blue-sky a share of the market you might be able to attract in the first year and in the first five years. Be realistic!

How are decisions made by potential customers? This is an especially difficult question to answer, but if you belong to any organizations whose members are already working with your potential customers, you might be able to get some help from them. Of special interest might be whether the decisions are made by a group, or whether one or just a few have the power to award you a contract. The more people involved in the decision-making process, the broader your marketing plan will have to be.

How many competitors do you have, and how difficult will it be to break in?

It will be important to know the strengths and weaknesses of the consultants you feel you might have to compete with for assignments. Also, see if you can determine how much of the total market each of the competitors currently has. How well established are they, and what would it take to lure away some of the assignments they now have? Would it be possible for you to get some sub-contracted assignments from some of these firms rather than trying to compete with them?

How expensive will it be for you to enter your chosen market? It's probably safe to assume that the amount of work in your area is already spoken for by the consultants with whom you will have to compete. This means that your marketing should either be aimed at generating work above the current level, or chipping away at business the other consultants have already sewn up. Either way, it will cost money to gain a foothold. It's a critical decision you will have to make.

What are the current market conditions like, and what are the short- and long-term conditions likely to be?

It will be necessary to have a grasp of the political, environmental, economic, social, and technological conditions that influence the potential of your business. Is this the right time to open a consulting business? Are there likely to be more people starting at the same time as you? What kind of pushback might you expect from the already-entrenched consultants? Are there other locations where the need for your services might be greater than your present location, and if so, would you be willing to relocate?

Will your anticipated pricing allow you to get a foothold?

There are many ways consultants can and do charge for their services, and I have discussed them in previous chapters. Now is the time to start thinking about how you can best price your services relative to market conditions, competition, and possible retaliation by established consultants. I have already mentioned that undercutting entrenched competitors is seldom a good plan. But what will work best for you? It's a decision only you can make. If you have answered the questions I have just posed, you should have a pretty good idea of what to do and what not to do.

If you have been able to answer all or most of these questions, chances are that you are beginning to see some patterns emerge. For example, suppose you see some strongly entrenched competition and a market for your services that is not expanding at a rate strong enough for you to pick up the untapped business. Under these circumstances, you might consider marketing your services to the larger consulting firms that dominate the field—firms that might welcome some help that wouldn't involve their adding the fixed expense of staff. This would give you immediate income and an opportunity to establish credentials and a reputation that could be put to better use in the future. Your marketing plan would, of course, be totally different than a plan to chip away at the well-established competitors.

On the other hand, suppose you find yourself in virgin territory with a major demand for the services you plan to offer. As a home-based individual consultant, you just might be seen as too small to handle the needs of potential clients. This, of course, calls for an entirely different marketing approach. You might even consider some strategic alliances with other consultants to make your fledgling company appear larger than life. Whatever you decide, your marketing plan would certainly be different than one you would use in a crowded field.

Putting the Pieces Together

If you have been able to answer the questions I have just posed, chances are good that you see some things coming together. Now it's time to start making some sense out of these answers. The better the image you have of your potential clients and their consulting needs, the more effective your marketing will be.

Picture Your Typical Client

You know what you can do, and you probably have a pretty good idea of the kind of help your potential clients might need. Now you need to start looking at potential clients from the point of view of how you might fit into their image of what a good consultant might be.

Some clients turn to consultants reluctantly, while others embrace them. Obviously those who are consultant-friendly go to the A list. Consultant-friendly clients see consultants as adjuncts with whom they work comfortably. On the other hand, some companies turn to consultants only when they fail to accomplish what they set out to do with their own staff. As long as you're pitching business, why not pitch it at the consultant-friendly crowd first. Lock up some of those early on, and you can pick and choose from the others later on.

Identify the Needs of Potential Clients

Consulting services are sought when a company needs services that cannot be provided by existing in-house staff. The help needed may be a rescue mission when problems arise that no one in-house can handle; or it may be an assignment to provide specialized services that the company does not want to staff up to do itself. Some consulting assignments are short, while others may involve long-term contractual arrangements. It's difficult to predict when a company will have problems and need your help; it's a lot easier to get a handle on what others are doing and how you might fit into their plans. Research the companies that might have a use for your services and try to determine specific areas where your services might be needed. If you can, talk with some of their suppliers to get an idea of what they are buying and doing. Check out the organizations they might belong to and see what might be available from them. In other words, learn as much as you can about your potential clients so you'll be ready to present your services to them in a way that shows them a consulting relationship with you would be a good and efficient fit. It's important to do this research before you make any calls on them. You want to arrive with ideas and answers, not questions about what they do!

Identify Your Competitors

It's not necessarily a bad sign when you uncover that there are a lot of consultants serving the companies you have identified as good prospects. This tells you that your prospects are accustomed to working with consultants, and that you don't have to sell them on the idea. That's one problem solved. The other is to discover just how to position yourself in order to fit in with the entrenched consultants. Don't be tempted to build your marketing strategy on undercutting the fees of your competitors. It may work in the short run, but seldom leads to anything more than immediate business, and few (if any) long-term relationships. Just keep in mind that your competitors have already been able to prove themselves to the clients. Your job is to get the opportunity to prove yourself in the face of established competition. I talk about this in detail in the next chapter. For now, to help you complete your marketing plan, do everything you can to get to know your competitors thoroughly.

Discover Your Competitive Strengths and Weaknesses

Once you know enough about your competitors, it's time to see where you stand competitively. There are bound to be areas you can exploit to your advantage, even when you might be facing larger and better-established competitors. As consulting firms get larger, they tend to look for larger and more complex assignments. In doing this, they often overlook and even avoid some of the smaller projects that you could handle, and that would give you the opportunity to get your foot in the door. Identify these projects and include them in your marketing plan.

A marketing plan is essentially a sequential program. And taking the small steps first is a safer and far better way to go than trying to get your fledgling company off the ground while keeping your head above water. If you can say that one of the major companies in your field is (or was) one of your clients, even though it may have been a small project, you will have a good hook for future pitches to other potential clients.

The Plan Itself

If you have been doing most of what I have been suggesting, you probably have piles of paper, books, and notes about each of the topics I have introduced. Now let's see how you can put them to use. It's time to get a bit more formal with your planning, but don't get obsessive about it. The best thing that can come out of this kind of planning is having a clear head about where you are competitively, where you want to go, and outlining a few ideas about how to get there.

At this point, you might want to start making notes as you go along. You should have a formal, but simple plan, it should be in writing, and it should serve as a flexible tool, not a straitjacket. Here we go!

Focus on Your Target Market

A tight focus is critical in the early stages of growing a new consulting business. Not only should you know the industries, companies, and types of people you would like to consult with, but you should also have a very clear picture of the businesses and people with whom you should *not* become involved. This is not always obvious to many new consultants who rush to get billing and take on clients that they should never work with. There's always a temptation to take an assignment that's offered simply because it represents immediate income. It might be better to borrow the money you need to keep open than to get involved with inappropriate clients.

Taking on an inappropriate client usually involves spending a lot of time just getting up to speed before you can do anything productive for the client. And it also means that your suggestions and recommendations may not be the best for the client. Always remember that most consulting business comes from recommendations, so be sure that whatever you take on will at the very least not damage your reputation.

A target focus is far more efficient than any scattershot approach to client acquisition. If you have researched the potential clients in your area, you should know more than just the fact you would be compatible with them. You should be aware of what they are doing, where they might be in any stage of project development, and just where and how you could plug into their work to best advantage. If you can visit with a potential client and start talking immediately about the project he or she is working on, you have already rounded second base.

Position Your Business Relative to Your Competitors

It's especially important to differentiate yourself and your business from the entrenched competitors. You have to show potential clients where you fit in, what you can do that other consultants may not do—or may not do as well as you—and why the prospect should take a chance on you.

Surprisingly, new (and small) consulting companies can often pitch and get business from clients that are already using larger and more well-known consultants, and I'm not talking about cutting price to get it. Most larger consultants take on smaller projects from existing clients more as an accommodation than for the fees involved. As a result, they are occasionally tempted to put junior staff on the smaller projects. Regardless of the ability of the juniors, some clients resent this. This, as you can surely see, is an opening begging to be exploited.

Once you have identified your list of potential clients and determined what some of your larger competitors might be doing for them, your knowledge of the field should give you the clues you need to make the most productive pitches. Incidentally, this is one of the reasons why larger consultants often sub out some projects to smaller consultants. This allows them to keep total control over their relationship with the client, and it also acts as a disincentive to the smaller subcontractor if he or she starts thinking big.

Create Your Own Referrals

Image is a critical factor in selling consulting services. It's not the kind of business that is sold by making cold calls. For want of a better word, it's just unprofessional. This is where networking really works well. Friends of friends, people you may never have met, probably know some of the people you should get to know. Put out the word, ask everyone, do whatever it takes to identify the names of real people at your key prospective clients. Remember, consulting is not a volume-based business. You only need a few good contacts to get started, and once started, the referrals are easy to get.

In addition to networking, use whatever media is appropriate to make an impression on potential clients. I'm not talking about extensive advertising—that seldom works, and when it does, it's rarely cost-effective. Think about writing articles for the publications that your prospects read. I talk about this in some detail in the next chapter. But for now, you should be noting this and any other ideas you might have for developing referrals to include in your marketing plan.

Pitfalls to Avoid

Your marketing plan, as you have probably gathered, does not have to be complex. It can be as formal as you like, but it's generally better to keep it simple, stick to any timetables you may have set up, and be prepared to make changes when they are necessary. There are, however, some pitfalls that await most new consultants, and this is a good time to discuss them. You might even want to include a "Don't Do" list in your plan if you feel that any of these pitfalls might await you.

Here are some of the pitfalls often mentioned by consultants:

Allowing a Potential Client to Talk You into Taking a Smaller Fee

The consultant who mentioned this feels strongly about presenting a professional image, and, as she put it, "Professionals don't cut price for any reason. If you really want the business, it's not uncommon to modify the terms of the engagement so that the client is more comfortable about the fee you have stated. For example, suppose you estimate that the work the client needs to have done will take you 200 hours and you have quoted a fee of $150 per hour. It's probably the total figure of $30,000 that is the problem, not your hourly rate. If you can suggest ways to modify the work of the engagement so that fewer hours would be involved, it will probably do the trick. And, it has the added benefit of showing the client that you are trying to accommodate him or her. It's usually easy enough to pare down some of the requirements to get to an acceptable price, rather than to push a deal that could evaporate." You might want to include several examples in your marketing plan of how you might modify certain conditions to get business, but not by altering your basic fee.

Communicating in "Consultanese," Not in the Language of Your Prospects

Every field has its lingo, and the better able you are to speak the language of your clients, the closer you are to getting engagements. More than just the buzzwords, you should be aware of the key issues in the field as they relate to the project you might be offered, and you should be able to discuss them intelligently. Don't try to overwhelm your client, even though you may be smarter than he is.

Not Really Seeing Yourself as Your Prospect Might See You

None of us really see ourselves as others do. You may think you're doing fine with a pitch, but the prospect might be seeing an entirely different image of you. None of your friends, even your good friends, will probably risk telling you that you are a bore or an overbearing person. If you get even the slightest hint of problems in this area, you might want to contact one of the many consultants and organizations that help people with their personal images. Toastmasters International can put you on the right track with your public speaking very quickly.

Frequently Asked Questions

1. *Just how flexible can a marketing plan be? Are there any rules that can be applied when changes seem necessary?*

   Changes should only be made when it's apparent that major opportunities or major problems are on the horizon. For example, if your focus has been on recruitment and staffing issues for clients and the economy has taken a major downward shift, it makes sense to add an outsourcing component to the services you offer, even if you didn't include that in your original marketing plan. It's best to avoid overreacting to small events unless you are seeing a lot of them, and they all point to the need for a possible shift in your marketing plan's focus.

2. *My hourly fee doesn't seem to be a problem with most of my clients, but I'm sure I could add a few more clients by offering a lower fee. So far, by sticking to the pricing structure of my marketing plan, business has grown steadily. Does this make sense?*

   It's probably not a good idea to have a two-tier pricing picture. If, as you say, most of your clients do not have a problem with your pricing, why not try to expand the penetration you have with those clients and be paid at your already-acceptable rate? If you really want to add clients who can't pay your higher fee, you might think about making a strategic alliance with another consultant who might be willing to work for less. Just make sure that your preferred clients know that you, yourself, are not working for a smaller fee.

3. *I have identified most of my potential competitors in my marketing plan;
    they are all independent companies of various sizes. Should I also include
    the companies that have their own internal consulting facilities?*
    It's not uncommon for some of the larger conglomerates to have internal
    consulting services that try to operate as impartial consultants for the com-
    panies and divisions within the corporate family. I wouldn't look at them as
    competitors, but as good sources of potential business. Many of these in-
    house consulting operations depend heavily on outside sources to complete
    certain assignments. They turn to them mainly when truly unbiased help is
    needed, when there is a need for talent they don't have on staff, and when
    they have more work than they can handle. More than a few smaller con-
    sulting firms do significant business with in-house consulting departments.
    You might want to switch these operations from your competitive list to the
    list of your target clients.

11 Promoting the Practice

Here's where we get into a minor semantic muddle. Most consultants you talk with will tell you that you can't sell consulting services by advertising. However, if you read any of the business journals, magazines, and newspapers, you will see ads for many consulting firms, both new and established. So, who's right and who's wrong? Neither one, as it turns out.

Those who answer reflexively that you can't sell consulting services by advertising are thinking of it as a retailer might think of running an ad for a sale. The retailer wants store traffic immediately. In that sense, advertising for immediate consulting business is far from cost-efficient. But, when you define advertising as a paid message in any appropriate medium to create an image that could lead to business in the future, you will begin to see that advertising is definitely an important promotional tool.

If definitions work for you, think of this as *public relations advertising*. You may be paying for the print ads or the on-air mentions, but your goal is long-term, rather than to turn up immediate business. Of course, if your ad happens to catch a prospect at the right time, such business could turn up immediately. The point is this: Whether you are new to the game or an old hand, don't rule out advertising; just be sure that you clearly define your goals.

If you have gone through the drill of the last chapter, you should have a pretty clear idea of who your prospects are, where to find them, and what you need to do to get their attention. This chapter is about doing just that, and more—turning prospects into clients. Before I get into the nuts and bolts of the process, let me finish what I started in the last chapter by talking about positioning.

Positioning Your Business for Maximum Advantage

However you choose to promote your business, you will probably be awash in a sea of competitors. You may face entrenched competitors who can probably outspend you to get new business. You will probably have to compete with others who are pretty much at the same point as you. The job you face is not just to get the business you need to keep going—it's to create an image that sets you apart from all the others and helps you get past the new-kid-on-the-block image. In short, you need to position your business relative to the needs of your prospects and in the context of your competitors' promotional quantity, quality, and intensity.

Even though a prospect may have never worked with a consultant before, chances are that they already have images of the consulting firms that serve their field. Their colleagues may have made suggestions; they have been exposed to advertising, promotion, and public relations programs that have already earned these other consultants a position in the prospect's mind. And here you are, wondering how you can not only get your foot in the door, but also position yourself for growth.

If you happen to be the first in your particular field to offer services that have been unavailable in the past, you pretty much own the field. However, this is seldom the case today. So, from here on, I'll be talking about positioning from the perspective of competitive activity.

You will probably discover that the competitor with the largest share of the business in your area was probably the first, or at least among the early consultants to set up shop. Just being there is a strong advantage. The major competitor may not necessarily be the best, but it has had the advantage of time in a field in which it did not have to compete. It's probably unwise to try to take on the leader head to head, but if you see that the number-one firm is spending a lot of time and money crowing about being number one, it's usually a good indicator that the firm is not feeling all that secure about its position. The company could be vulnerable, and you just might be able to take away some of the marbles.

Most consulting companies get their start pretty much the same way you are getting yours—they started with a specialty, and gradually grew by adding other services until they became what they are today: broad-based consulting firms. They have gone from the position of being a specialized firm to one that covers many bases.

This makes good sense from the perspective of a growing firm, but it also leaves them vulnerable to incursions by new consultants whose focus is narrow and tightly

Spotting Competitive Openings

It's often possible to take business from larger and more firmly entrenched competitors, but you have to be sure of yourself, and you have to know just which aspect of the competitors' activity is vulnerable. Just as you know your own strengths and weaknesses, you must have an equally clear picture of your competitors' strengths and weaknesses. The buzz in any field should give you at least a general idea of your competitors' weak spots, but you should confirm your findings before you take that big step. And, of course, it could be a big mistake to actually point out your competitors' weaknesses to a prospect directly. Stress what you do that is better, and lead the prospect to draw his or her own conclusions. When you have a clear idea of the obstacles you might face, you can tailor your promotion accordingly. Some of the best opportunities for new consultants to challenge bigger competitors come during times of economic slowdown, when new technology appears and when the political climate shifts noticeably.

targeted. The bigger a consulting firm gets, the greater the overhead it has to support. It seldom happens that all divisions of multifunction consulting firms are equally profitable. This, then, usually leads the firm to focus on the centers that produce the most revenue, and to slight the others. And here's where you can usually spot opportunities if your specialty is one that is not being aggressively supported by the larger firms in your field.

The job, then, is to position yourself as *the* specialist in an area that is less likely to attract retaliation by the larger competitor, and where you can gain a strong foothold. The larger firm may even be happy to have someone take over the particular small niche they once controlled. You will probably only see some competitive pushback if and when you start to expand and your big competitor starts seeing you as a growing threat; it all depends on your personal plans. You just might be able to build a very solid business by positioning yourself as the focused expert to your clients while still not a big threat to your competitors. If you have big plans, you're going to have to think differently. But, from the perspective of this book, I'm assuming that your goal is (and probably should be) just to get started, get into the black, and discover what you can and can't do effectively and with limited capital.

Going for Second Place

The specialty approach is not for everyone. It can be limiting, and you are often more vulnerable to competitors than might be the more broad-based consulting firms. If this is your thinking, consider positioning yourself as number two to the leading competition. This, of course, is not the path to follow if number one in your area is a firm like McKinsey & Company. But suppose that the number-one spot is occupied by a capable, but somewhat larger firm, and that there is a real possibility you could someday compete with them for the top spot.

The best approach is not to compete head-on, but to position yourself as the number-two firm. In a way, this approach is a lot like taking the specialty position, except that you will be offering more than specialty services. You should look for an area of service that number one is weak in, or has intentionally neglected, and try to fill the vacuum. Make no mistake: Your competitor will not ignore you, so be prepared to defend yourself and to aggressively go after more than just the neglected specialty business.

The consultants who go this route are generally considered boutique shops. That is, they are small versions of larger shops, and not just firms with a tightly focused specialty. The appeal of the boutique approach for potential clients usually lies in the firm's ability to take on and complete assignments a lot faster that the larger competitor.

The firms that are often most successful with this approach are those that don't spend a lot of time, money, and effort building a particular image, but do focus on getting potential clients to think about their competitors in different ways. You don't call specific attention to yourself, but you do call attention to your competitor in ways that reflect positively on your own company. No, I'm not talking about mudslinging, but I am talking about the subtle techniques that change perceptions without starting an outright competitive war.

A typical example of how this can be done might be writing and placing an article about the advantages a smaller consulting firm (like yours, of course) has over its larger competitors. These stories are usually based on specific case histories that are especially meaningful to the prospects you have in mind for growing your business. Being number two is not a bad place to be, and many an astute consultant has turned down opportunities to do what has to be done to get the number-one slot. Think of the win, place, and show structure of horse-race betting; if you know anything about the odds and the payoffs, the picture gets a lot clearer.

Naming Your Firm

An appropriate name for your company is important, and coming up with the right name is not all that easy. It's usually better to have a name that tells prospects something about what you do. However, such a name can be limiting as you grow and take on more and varied work. It's tempting to use acronyms, but this is usually best done after your company has already become established, when people would recognize what the letters stood for. IBM obviously stands for International Business Machines Corporation. But, if the founder had called the firm IBM right from the start, it would have meant nothing to anyone.

The most practical approach is to use your own name and follow that name with a tagline that is easily changed as the direction of your business changes. For example, James Green Consulting as a main name says that you are a consulting firm. A line slugged under the registered name might say, "Consulting to Book Publishers." The second line is descriptive and can be changed as you grow. In the meantime, James Green Consulting continues to do what it is meant to do—build name recognition. If you expand in the future, you can simply change the tagline to something like: "Consulting to Book and Periodical Publishers."

Aim for something descriptive, but avoid getting into a name trap that would make it difficult for you to move easily into different fields. Many of the big management consulting firms got their start in accounting. As they saw opportunities, they expanded into areas that were open to them and logical from the point of view of their client base. If any of them had had the word "accounting" in their names, it would have posed a problem when they expanded their services.

Publicity, Promotion, and Public Relations

Publicity, promotion, and public relations are the three tools that are most productive not only for launching a consulting business, but also for growing and expanding it. There are no hard lines that divide the three, and what some might call publicity, others might call public relations. So, here's how I use the terms in this chapter:

Publicity

Publicity is an intentional attempt to create or change an audience's views on a specific subject. As I use it here, publicity is a tool of public relations that usually makes use of free exposure in the media which covers a target audience. A press release sent to the publication that reaches your potential clients and published at no charge is a typical example of publicity. The most productive use of publicity is to spread the word about newsworthy events that concern you, your business, or even your clients, when you are part of the material. Publicity is timely information about you and your business.

Promotion

Like publicity, promotion usually involves an attempt to place material with the media that will reach your potential clients without charge, although promotion is usually not as time-sensitive as is most publicity. A publicity release may announce that you have just been nominated for some award in your field, while a promotional project is not necessarily breaking news, and usually appears as longer articles about topics of interest to all in your field. Promotion is seldom time-sensitive; while it may address timely subjects, it's not breaking news.

Public Relations

Public relations should be thought of as the overarching plan that creates and manages the development and placement of publicity and promotion. In addition to seeking placement of material in print and electronic media, a public relations program should also include attempts to get you live and personal exposure with those who might be good prospects for your services. The main tool here is booking speaking engagements and writing effective speeches. In many ways, speaking engagements are often the best way to get new business, and I'll explain why shortly.

Successful Implementation of Your PR Campaign

News about you, your company, and what you are doing for your clients in the appropriate media is one of the best ways to keep the name of your company in front of your prospects. Just make sure that the press releases and media contacts you make have real and current interest. If you recycle old stuff and send material that is only of tangential interest to a media editor, your material will probably be sidetracked before it's ever read. Once you get a good reputation with the editor of the journal that covers your field, or the business editor of your local newspaper, you will stand a good chance of having fairly regular exposure. The more a prospect sees your name or the name of your firm, the more likely it is that you'll be called when your services are needed.

If you need help with a press release, check with a local public relations agency or consult one of the many books on the subject. Be sure, however, to contact an agency that knows something about your field. If you are consulting with high-tech firms, a PR agency that specializes in retail promotions is not the place to be. The main strength of a good public relations agency is the contacts it has with the media, and how they can be put to use for you.

If you already have these contacts and want to write your own releases, just read the releases that each publication has been carrying and follow the dominant style of each medium. The traditional Who, What, When, Where, and How format is always a good place to start. Don't try to be creative!

Creating Effective Promotional Material

The best way to get critical attention for your firm is by seeking to have longer and more complex material published about you and your business. This is not the fast-breaking news of publicity; it should be a thought-provoking piece, or a piece that will be helpful to prospects over the long run.

One of the best ways is to do a survey of some of the key people in your field on a subject that will be of interest to your prospects, and to write an article based on the results for a magazine or blog that reaches your prospects. The chief advantage of this approach is that you get your name and the name of your company attached to the names of key figures in the field. It's not easy to get these people to spend the time needed for in-depth articles, but most are usually willing to either answer a few survey questions or to give you a few cogent lines that you can quote in your article.

Most media prefer to be queried first rather than to be sent a finished article. These publications can often provide helpful guidance as well as contact information that you may not be able to get on your own. Others are willing to consider material already written, but you may be asked to make some changes and additions if the editors are looking for more information or a different slant. You can usually get this information just by sending a short e-mail to the editors who are interested in your type of material. Just ask for a copy of their editorial guidelines to be sent by return e-mail, and you will have everything you need to get started.

Other promotional material usually includes a printed promotional brochure and a Web site. Both usually require professional help. Nothing can sink you faster that clumsy promotion, whether it's on paper or on the Web. Before you call any of these professionals, however, see if you can get copies of your key competitors' promotional material. It's important to review this material to see just where each might be vulnerable and where your promotional efforts can help get your foot in the door. Your Web designer or ad agency may be the best in the business, but this has to be a collaborative effort; it has to reflect not only the facts about your business, but also the human side of your enterprise. Without that part of the equation, any promotion you do will probably look like a laundry list of your skills. Consulting is a very personal business, and it's important for whoever creates your print material or Web site to create a picture of you as an accessible and personable consultant, as well as one who is fully capable of understanding his clients' issues.

Writing and Giving a Good Speech

Most successful consultants will probably tell you that some of their best and most productive clients came to them as a result of having seen and heard them give a speech or deliver a professional paper. Today, more than ever, a consultant needs to be a public person in order to really prosper. While appearing in print is important, a speech gives you the opportunity to be seen immediately. Most consultants will tell you that a good speech is the equivalent of pitching a room full of prospects simultaneously. And when you do get the call for an initial meeting, all the preliminaries are already out of the way. The client has been pre-sold, and it becomes pretty much a matter of getting right down to a specific project discussion.

Promoting Your Services on the Internet

The Internet is an excellent tool if you use it right. As long as you think of it as a prospecting and not a selling tool, you will be okay. Most of what you see about selling on the Internet is aimed at people who are trying to move products, not services. However, the Internet does stack up nicely as a prospecting tool, and it should be included as part of your overall program.

What has been said about placing news releases and articles applies equally as well to the Internet. You are probably already familiar with the Web sites, blogs, and other Internet postings that your prospects probably check regularly. Your job is to discover what has been on these sites and what is currently appearing on them, and then to discover just what each requires you to do to place a news release or an article. The key point to remember is that whatever you put on the Net, it should be designed to first, get a prospect's attention; second, it should help the prospect in some way; and third, it should include all of your relevant contact information.

I would strongly urge you to start a blog of your own in which you invite comments, positive and negative, about topics of interest to your prospects. This kind of interaction is producing business for more and more consultants, both large and small. You don't have to be well known to have your say on a blog that also includes some of the heavies in your field. In a way, this kind of interaction is a great leveler and a boon for the smaller consultant. You will quickly see that what you say about the blog topic is far more important than whether or not you are a new kid on the

Meet Jim Holtje . . .

Jim Holtje is chief speechwriter for Siemens Corporation, the international firm whose products include everything from railroad systems and major medical diagnostic machines to lightbulbs. And, yes, Jim is my son, for full disclosure. His five published books include *The Manager's Lifetime Guide to the Language of Power*, published by Prentice Hall. I asked Jim how a new consultant can best maximize his or her time on the podium. Here's what he told me.

"When a consultant is a guest speaker, everyone assumes that he or she is there to make a good impression and do a subtle pitch for business. And here's where most consultants fall on their face. No matter how hard they try, their obvious intentions show through quickly, and they are simply tolerated until they are off stage and the next speaker is introduced. The advice I give to inexperienced speakers is to address the subject as cleanly as possibly. That is, don't try to make the obvious references to how you solved a problem. Tell your listeners what they want to hear and need to hear. The very fact that there's no 'commercial' speaks far more loudly than any pitch, no matter how cleverly buried it might be in the text. Then, of course, be sure to have copies of your talk along with your business card to give out to the attendees. Most talks include a question and answer session. Be sure to get the names and contact information of those who ask questions. This gives you an immediate and good reason to phone them later. Simply tell them that you wanted to explain something else that you didn't have time for during the Q&A session, and the chances are very good that you will have an entree very quickly."

If you are not a comfortable speaker, take the time to learn how to do it and do it well. Most of the consultants I know went from major stage fright to being comfortable speakers after either getting some professional help or stumbling on their own until they got their stage legs. There's an added benefit to getting comfortable as a speaker, and that's the fact that it will help you when your assignment includes addressing and interacting with client groups. You'll be surprised at how quickly you can go from jitters to actually looking forward to being onstage.

block or an old and experienced one. Discover the blogs and sites in your field and start taking an active part in them. Don't try to be a smart-ass, however. You may feel good about one-upping someone else, but that's not the point. The point is to position yourself as someone who can be turned to for answers and help. Get a bad rep on the Net, and the doors you want to open will get very sticky!

Frequently Asked Questions

1. *I have worked from a home office for years, and never had a client express concern over this. Is it worth the effort to promote the fact that when someone works with me, I'm the consultant they will work with, not some junior?*
   It's not a good selling point. Not that you should hide the fact that you work from home, but this just isn't a benefit to a prospect. The key to good promotion is hitting hard on the points that are important to your prospects. It seems that you are probably already doing this from what you said, so stick with what you are doing. Change is fine, but not just for its own sake.

2. *I would like to write an article for a magazine that most of my prospects read regularly, but the few letters I have written to the editor have not moved him to ask for the piece. Are there any tricks I can use?*
   This isn't exactly a trick; it's pretty much what professional writers do when they query magazine editors about articles. Rather than write a cover letter, write the first few paragraphs of the article you plan to write and lead into a final short paragraph asking him or her if it would work for the magazine. Your lead—the opening paragraph—should not only identify the subject and the problem to be discussed, but it should also demonstrate a level of writing that the editor knows will not have to be heavily worked over.

12 | Expanding Your Business

A home-based business is usually a labor of love—something you do mainly because you really like the work and you want to build something for yourself. Few do it because they envision selling it someday, but many see their businesses outgrowing the home office. At the moment, however, you are probably still trying to put wheels on your wagon and haven't given much thought to what you might do with the business later. Your notion of expansion at the moment is probably limited to reaching the point where the business is in the black and you can cut back to a six-day week. However, as busy as you might be cranking the business up, you should at least have some idea of what you can do with a business down the road.

This chapter and the next will address the decisions you will face later—to maintain your original idea of working from a home office, expanding beyond the limitations of a home office, and finally, selling the business. How you see your later years now will help you plan in an orderly fashion, and will probably prevent you from making some serious mistakes. This isn't really a big deal, especially since you probably have your hands full at the moment growing your business. But stick with me through these last two chapters; you won't regret it!

Growing a Home-Based Business

A consulting business is quite different from just about any other business that can be run from a home office. The business is you. It's you who holds hands with clients. It's you who does the research, writes the reports, and implements the suggestions you make. Sure, you may have some part-time help, and maybe even have set up some appropriate strategic alliances with other consultants and services. But it's you the clients think of when they give you assignments. Take a sick day, go on vacation, or just don't reply to a client's call for a few days, and you will soon see just how critical you are to your business.

This means that you must manage your time better than you ever did when you worked for someone else, and you must have established relationships with clients that allow you some flexibility—and even a little private life. For many this isn't a problem, but for those whose experience has mainly been working for someone else, this can be a difficult transition.

The first few years of running a home-based consultancy is a shakedown cruise of your business ship. You'll find some leaks in the hull that need to be repaired. The engines will be balky until they are properly run in. And the hull will take a pounding from anxious clients and aggressive competitors. But, by the time you realize that your ship is seaworthy, you will be on a good course and focused mainly on getting enough work to meet your projections, plus a bit more to say that you are growing.

If you are like most consultants, you will view your business in terms of your billable hours, or the time needed to complete quoted projects. What's left over is the time you need to fill with more business for that wonderful comfort zone when the engines are running well, but not straining; when the hull plates hold during an occasional storm; and when the deck is secure from competitive attack.

Going from Up-and-Running to Successful

Whether you are running your home-based consulting business part-time or are working at it full-time, there will come a point when you have to decide what to do with the business. If it just isn't making it regardless of what you do to promote it, you may have to close down and possibly try again later. But, if the business has caught on, you face another set of issues.

If you're doing it part-time, you will probably have to decide whether to continue part-time or work at it full-time. There are far too many business and personal issues to address here, but in general, a decision to go full-time should be made only after careful planning and research on the current state of your field and its growth potential for you. Nothing is foolproof, but with good planning, you will have a far better chance of succeeding than if you go at it blindly.

It's important to know just what you want to achieve with your business. Do you see it mainly as an adjunct to the income you get from your full-time work, or do you see it turning into your full-time work? You may even be in that fortunate position of having a part-time business take off to the point where you either have to make the move, or cut back and possibly lose some of the part-time clients who seem to need what you have to offer. Remember—you can't turn down many assignments before clients see the need for more reliable help and turn to others to provide that help.

For now, let's assume that no one is breaking down the doors, but that you have managed to get some good clients who like your work, and you know that there is enough other business for you to make a go of it full-time. Consultant Marc Dorio tells me that he has resisted the temptation of growing a bigger business. As he puts it, "The bigger a business gets, the less personal it gets. Whether you want to expand or remain small is a very personal decision. The larger you get, the less you will do of the work that got you into your own business in the first place. If you really enjoy that work, running a larger business may not be for you. I happen to enjoy my work very much, and I have been able to make my consulting business work well for me without expanding, so I tend to favor this approach. I have friends who do the same work as I who have expanded dramatically and are just as happy running a larger firm. It's what makes them happy. There are no answers that fit everyone. You really have to get a handle on just who you are and what you want from life, and take the appropriate path."

Marc has had his own one-person home-based business for over twenty years, and counts major commercial as well as institutional organizations among his clients. The fact that he works from home has never been a problem for him or for any of his clients. Here are a few questions that Marc suggests you ask yourself when you are at the point of deciding just how big you would like your consulting business to be.

Why Should You Expand Your Business?

If there are opportunities to be seized, that's one thing. If the business is your full-time livelihood, that's another. But in either case, the real decision is just how much expansion is possible if you plan to stay a small, home-based business, or if your goal is to ramp up to something a lot larger. Remember that a small business will usually remain fragile, no matter how successful you are, simply because *you* are the business. A larger business can be less fragile, but it can become a cash-eating machine if you are not careful. As Marc puts it quite succinctly, "If you like the idea of supporting a payroll and managing a business more than doing the work of the business, then by all means go for the growth. On the other hand, if you can satisfy your personal goals without taking on the responsibilities growth implies, then staying small is the way to go. Don't let friends and even relatives try to influence your decision. This is something you will work very hard at long after the decision has been made."

Marc does point out, however, that there is another alternative for the person who would like to grow a bigger business, but who really prefers to remain at the forefront of the client work being done. "Think about hiring support people to allow you to continue to do the work that gives you pleasure. A few good part-time people who handle all the details of your business while you do the client work is a really good way to go."

Should You Expand Your Service Base or Keep a Narrow Focus?

Most home-based consultants get their start by offering a specialized service directly to clients, or by subcontracting work from larger consulting firms. Growth depends on the need for the services you offer, the current competition, the cost of expansion, and the long-term potential for the services you offer. Here are a few questions you need to ask before you make any big decisions:

- Which of your present services are the most profitable?
- Is there a growing need for your number-one service?
- Can you sell more of your number-one service to your present client base, or will you have to grow by seeking new clients?
- What related services can you sell to your present clients?
- Is there a growing need for a service that you can perform that might eclipse the need for the service or services you currently sell?
- What will it cost to expand the services you offer to present clients, as well as to expand by seeking new clients?
- Will any of your expansion plans require outside help or expanded facilities —either an office outside your home, or an expansion of your present home office?
- What are the short- and long-term investment requirements for any expansion you might consider?

Here's where you have to pull out your business plan and your marketing plan. Both should contain information that will inform your decisions. Probably the most critical decisions you will have to make will involve money. You will need to know whether you can expand with existing capital, or whether you will have to borrow money to do it. If your business is part-time and you don't depend on the income for routine living expenses, you might be able to finance an expansion simply by plowing consulting income back into the business. However, this can take a lot longer than if you were to invest directly and possibly with borrowed capital. Be sure you assess all the personal and business risks in any decisions you make.

How Big Can a Home-Based Consulting Business Get?

Part-time backup is usually available everywhere. Bookkeepers, clerical staff, and even semiprofessional assistants are usually readily available to either work right in your office, or as independent contractors from their own home offices. Help from this quarter will get you to the point where you can maximize the time you put into the business, whether it's a part-time shop or a full-time operation. However, what happens when you are overworked professionally?

You may have staff taking care of the details, but you are the person who performs the services the clients pay for. This is where most small consultancies are most vulnerable to making mistakes, or plain bad decisions. The owners see potential for growth, but they are unsure about the best way to go. It's where you are really tested about your commitment to remaining a small, home-based business. Since this is a book about home-based consulting businesses, I'll pass on the potential of turning a home-based business into a larger business that must operate from outside the home and focus on a system that has allowed many to build large and profitable practices while still operating from a home office—the strategic alliance.

Growing Your Business with Strategic Alliances

Basically, a strategic alliance is two or more organizations working together to achieve a common goal. This, however, is more than just a buzz phrase. It's more than two consultants simply helping each other out on an as-needed basis, and the word *strategy* is the defining concept. A strategy is a long-term plan, and by forming strategic alliances, many consultants have leveraged their positions greatly. Each counts on the other for something specific. In some cases an alliance between two consultants involves filling skill gaps; in others, it involves providing backup when one of the consultants has an overload of work. In all cases, it requires a willingness

A Case in Point

A network of strategic alliances is not seen by clients the same way as a large consulting firm with regional offices is seen. However, this is seldom a problem for the smaller firms or individuals of a network of alliances when they work together to promote the potential of the network, as well as their own interests. Each of the members of the alliance must be comfortable with and supportive of all the other members of the alliance. For example, the editors who formed The Consulting Editors Alliance are not only comfortable working with people with whom they might compete for projects, but they also actively refer work to each other. As alliance member Danelle McCafferty says, "Because of our diverse experience, we are able to provide services in many areas." Each of the members of this alliance has a specialty, yet each is capable of providing services in most other editorial fields. On the surface, this might seem to be a recipe for a witch's brew, but it is probably one of the best examples I've seen of consultants cooperating for their mutual benefit as well as for their own individual advantage.

to work closely together, even when you might also be competing in each other's areas. In short, it requires a rather high level of trust between or among the participants. Although there might appear to be a lot of room for mischief, very few consultants seem to have had bad experiences with these alliances. The more common complaint seems to be that one of the partners was unable to perform as "advertised." But, this is no reason to avoid considering them when the need arises. What is required, then, is a thorough understanding of each other's abilities and skills.

Surprisingly, one of the major reasons consultants cite for becoming involved in strategic alliances is not to ramp up billing, but to take advantage of growing international opportunities, and to fend off competitors. More than a few of the well-known management consultants have greatly expanded their international reach by forming strategic alliances. This has been a very productive way for many to gain a presence in smaller countries where the cost to operate their own branch might be prohibitive. This means that an expansion could occur by being the strategic partner of an offshore consulting firm seeking a presence in the United States.

For the moment, however, let's talk about strategic alliances from the perspective of growing your nascent firm locally or regionally. If you think in terms of limiting your risk and maximizing your professional leverage, you are on the right track. A good strategic alliance will allow you to extend your professional reach without having to invest in a bigger payroll. In a sense, you will have the talent you need on demand, as will your strategic partner. Here are the major benefits any consulting firm, large or small, will have with carefully planned and executed strategic alliances:

- You will have more to offer clients, and you will add a competitive advantage when you solicit new business.
- A good strategic alliance can broaden the scope of the market for your services.
- It's possible to become an "international" firm with one or more offshore strategic alliances.
- You can ratchet up your image when competing for clients that you might not be able to go after otherwise.
- You and your alliance partner can combine skills and ideas that will result in services that neither of you could have offered individually before the alliance.
- You can "expand" without investing the money it would take to do so by the conventional means of hiring staff and getting larger quarters.

How to Form a Strategic Alliance

Strategic alliances can be and are sometimes formed just to take advantage of a specific opportunity of benefit to both partners. A marketing consultant may have an immediate need for market research, and rather than take on the research work, he might combine forces with a research consultant for the one-time project. This is how consultants are often introduced to the concept. From our perspective, however, strategic alliances are tools of expansion. They are planned carefully and specifically to grow a business. So, for what follows, think of these alliances as growth plans, not as short-term relationships. These are the steps most often involved in a planned alliance:

Making the Decision to Expand with a Strategic Alliance

Whether you are at the point of turning away business or still looking to add billable hours to your week, the decision to grow by strategic alliance is as serious as growing by hiring and expanding facilities. It's not as expensive, of course, but the personal and business consequences of a troubled strategic alliance can be just as damaging as those you might encounter in a conventional expansion. The first step is to set specific objectives for the alliance, and to have a very clear image of the type of consultant with whom you might form an alliance. Focus on the facilities you have and those you would like to add by way of an alliance. Have a definite idea of what you expect a partner to bring to the table and what you are prepared to offer in exchange.

Define the Partner You Would Like to Have

Before you ever investigate specific partner possibilities, have a very clear image of the type of firm you would feel comfortable working with; focus not only on the professional skills needed, but also on the personalities of the people with whom you would feel most comfortable. Be aware that you will probably have to be somewhat flexible in both categories. Perfect people just don't exist. This means that you should build some slack into the picture you have of the perfect alliance partner. Remember: A person willing to partner with you may have totally different reasons for seeking an alliance than you have, but as long as you share common goals, you will be on the right track. I have met partner consultants who are so far apart politically that it's hard to imagine the alliance working, but it does. They just don't push each other's political buttons.

Define Your Alliance Terms Very Carefully

You should draw up either a thorough letter of agreement or a formal contract. You may want to make a first draft yourself, but I urge you to seek the services of an attorney who has had experience with similar situations. Before you talk to an attorney, you and your prospective partner should have long and detailed discussions about what each of you hope to get out of the relationship, and what you are willing to put into it. You should pay particular attention to how you will resolve competitive issues. Will you share proprietary or competitive information? How will each of you be compensated for the work that the alliance is being formed to do? How will you resolve conflicts? How will you terminate the relationship? It's really best to discuss and resolve these issues right from the start.

Define How the Alliance Will Be Managed

Your alliance will, in effect, have two co-equal bosses. That's usually a prescription for disaster, but if you handle the management issues, relative to each partner's interest in the projects, you will greatly reduce the potential for conflict. Who will manage the money, and how will it be managed? Will the alliance be set up with its own bank account, or will each member bill according to his or her participation in client activity? What about backup costs? And this just scratches the surface. Although it's easier to get out of a failed alliance, the fallout can have serious effects on you and your business.

Calling It Quits

Most strategic alliances don't end in rancorous disagreement, but because one of the partners moves on to other things, including retirement. Either way, however, your agreement should describe how things will be settled when it's over. As I mentioned, some strategic alliances are formed for specific projects and are dissolved when the project has been completed. But when an alliance is formed with long-term goals in mind, a dissolution, for whatever reason, should be based on terms each partner has already agreed to.

A Strategic Alliance Should Be Based on More than Just a Handshake

Unless you see an alliance as being infrequent periods of mutually agreed-upon cooperation, you should probably set up a more formal arrangement. It's not uncommon for two or more consultants to participate in a joint venture, in which each consultant owns an agreed-upon number of shares (if the corporate structure is used). This can be done by individuals, or, if each party is a corporation, the corporations can own the shares. Either way, there is equity involved as well as certain responsibilities that the corporate form demands. As long as you know what might be possible to help expand your business, you will be in a better position to plan for the future.

If your needs and the needs of the others you are considering an alliance with are less complex, you would probably be better served by establishing a nonequity strategic alliance. This is done simply by contractual arrangement among the partners, describing all the details of participation, but without actually forming a separate company. There are advantages and disadvantages to both, but they are better explained by your lawyers when you have all your needs and requirements clearly stated.

Frequently Asked Questions

1. *I currently have significant opportunities for my services (i.e., executive development) in locations that are too far away for me to handle from my home office. What are the major problems of opening a branch office?*
    The first decision you have to make is which form of organization your expansion will take. This assumes that you have done your homework and have a good handle on the potential market and the operational costs in the areas in which you plan to expand. An expansion of your present business implies that you will hire people and take on the expense of office locations. If you look for strategic alliances with individuals already operating in the areas, you will not have these expenses. The question, then, is how much risk are you willing to take, and how comfortable do you feel about working with people over whom you will have little control? After that, it's more or less the same issues you would face with any other kind of a start-up.

2. *My field is market research, and I already have a successful one-person, home-based consulting business. Lately I have been approached by a few existing clients to consult on market development issues. I have the capability to do this, but is it a wise move for a one-person consulting firm to broaden focus like this?*

That would depend a lot on how you see the potential for your existing services. If it is expanding, or at least stable, it may not be a good move, unless you could partner with someone to take on the market development assignments. If your plans are to stay focused, it's probably better to own a small niche business rather than to go the bigger-is-better route. You don't have to be a "big" firm to have a good reputation.

3. *Is there any way that is better than others to expand into a new field?*
Probably the most effective and well-proven way to move into another field is to do a study of a specific issue of interest to potential clients and publish the results in an article in one of the periodicals that covers the field. A published article confers the title of expert and should at least get you in to see some potential clients. At that point, it's up to you to convince the client that you are the consultant for the work they need to have done. An expansion is best done when the field you plan to move in to is closely related to your present field. A wild jump is a bad risk.

13 | How to Sell Your Business

This chapter is about how to sell your business, but first, let's look at *why* you might want to sell it. As you probably guessed, most small consultancies are sold because the owners would like to retire. Another reason many give is that someone made them an offer they could not refuse. And, of course, some go on the market because the founder either isn't making it, or for other personal reasons wants to get out.

Whatever your reason, you should realize that a consultancy, or almost any other personal service business, is difficult to sell. As the cliché goes, the major asset walks out the door at the end of every day. This pretty much rules out the idea of starting a business for the sole purpose of growing it and selling it. But it certainly shouldn't deter you from starting a consulting business. If you plan ahead, there are many things you can do as you build your business to make it more salable when and if you want to get out. And because it's possible to do very well in the field, it may not be necessary for your endgame strategy to consider a sale at all. Hard work, prudent investing, and some luck could leave you in a position to close the doors without selling the business at all.

Before we look at how your business might be sold, let's take a look at why someone might want to buy a home-based consulting business:

- You own a niche that other consultants have not been able to gain a foothold in
- You are seen as a competitor who could be neutralized by a strategic acquisition
- You have contacts that might take a competitor too long or be too expensive to win over

- The work you do would give another consultant contact leverage for the services they now offer

These are the factors that make most small consulting firms interesting to other firms. Now, here are some of the questions a prospective buyer will ask:

- Will the owner stay with the firm long enough to ensure that a solid transition takes place?
- If the owner has been scaling back in anticipation of retiring, can the downward trend be reversed, even if the original owner stays on?
- What guarantees can the original owner give that the current clients will remain with the firm after the sale?
- Will the owner sell to another firm if the deal isn't made, and how will this affect the competitive picture?
- Is it really necessary to buy the company at all?
- Are the profit margins in line with the margins of the acquiring firm? If adjustments upward are necessary, how much of the business that comes with the purchase might be lost?

Not all home-based consulting businesses stay the same as they grow. Many get started, succeed, and are expanded beyond the home-based style either by being acquired or by acquiring another business and moving to larger and commercially based quarters. In any case, the founder—the company's chief asset—stays with the merged business. In the previous chapter I discussed strategic alliances for expansion. Often these strategic alliances morph into formal business relationships that combine the strengths and energies of all those involved into a new company. Keep this in mind as you grow, but for now, our attention is on the best ways to sell your home-based consulting business.

Five Steps to the Successful Sale of Your Business
Before you make a move, think about whether you want to sell the business yourself, or whether you might want a business broker to handle the sale and all necessary transactions. You will surely need to work with your accountant and your lawyer.

Typically, business brokers ask for a 10 percent commission on the sale price if it's a million dollars or less. Most have a descending commission scale as the purchase price gets larger. These rates vary from business to business, so it's a good idea to

> **Business Sale Tip . . .**
>
> One of the first things a prospective buyer's accountant will do is check to see if you are up-to-date with your tax payments. If you are unable to make a current payment, file for an extension. Don't make it look like you're dodging a tax bullet.

talk with several brokers before you make a choice. Keep in mind that while a smaller commission rate is always attractive, it's the skill and experience record of the broker that should be the key element in your decision.

Selling a business is not an easy task, even when you have a business broker working on your case. Even though you may have reached the point where you do want to retire and don't have the enthusiasm you had when you built the business, don't let your guard down as you go through the sale process. Without proper attention, you just might leave too much on the table, and in your hurry to be off to the golf course you could very well commit yourself to details that you will regret later.

Be Specific About Why You Want to Sell Your Business

People who buy businesses are usually very concerned about the "real" reason someone wants to sell a business. "Why would someone want to sell a business that is this profitable?" is a common question business brokers are asked. Even when the real reason is retirement, it seldom satisfies buyers who might be committing a significant amount of their own money to the acquisition. This means that you should not only be personally honest about your reasons, but also that you should be prepared to carefully document all the benefits and problems that will go with the acquisition. Your accountant should be able to document all the figures to a prospect's satisfaction, but you must be able to tell your story honestly and convincingly.

If it's just too much work for one person, be honest about it. Your view of what is too much work might not frighten someone else. If you are having employee or alliance disputes, be honest about them. Apart from the importance of being truthful, if you don't reveal what's going on, you could be open to charges of falsification of information. If you are selling because you have not achieved the success or profit levels you envisioned, be honest about it. But be sure to detail exactly what you *have* done to get where you stand now. A prospective buyer may see that you are on the verge of better business, but you may just be worn out from trying.

Setting a Price for Your Business

The usual equations for determining the value of a small business are not especially helpful when it comes to selling a consulting business, especially a one-person business. The formula, based on multiples of current profits, often boils down to a multiple of one. This means that your sale price, if you can find a buyer, will be just what your most recent annual profit was. By contrast, a business that could do without the present owner and which had a long and successful history of growth might be priced at as much as ten times current profits. But there are ways to sell a one-person business—and to command a better than one-to-one sale price—and I will get to that shortly.

Determining the Best Time to Sell Your Business

As with planning for growth, you should plan well ahead and carefully for the sale of your business—at least a year in advance is advised. By the time you start thinking about retiring, if this is your reason for selling, you have probably already slowed down a bit, and the change in momentum will be noticeable in the financials and other records a prospect would expect from you prior to a sale. Kick the wheel a bit harder. Bring in a few new clients. Get some good media exposure for the business. In short, make it look as attractive to a prospective buyer as you can. It may take a year or more to create the kind of salable image needed, so timing is critical.

If you have the luxury of time and your business is cyclical and predictable, plan to look for buyers during the upside of the cycle. Bring in a few new clients and try

Business Sale Tip . . .

Go over your tax returns for the past few years and see where it might be necessary to add back any discretionary expenses you might have made, such as a bumped-up salary in a particular year, and possibly even an automobile expense. A prospective buyer's accountant will want to know what the real costs of running the business are.

to get a few additional assignments from current clients. The business should look good—and so should you. Your enthusiasm will be critical, too. "I really don't want to quit, but the family says it's time for me to play more golf," tells a prospective buyer that he or she just might be in the same position in a few years. Play it for all it's worth.

Sell It Yourself or Get Some Professional Help

If an offer hasn't arrived on your desk unsolicited, you will have to decide whether to sell it yourself, or get the help of a business broker. Remember that either way, you will need the advice of an attorney and an accountant. Most small consulting businesses are usually sold to friends, competitors, or at least someone that the present owner knows. If no one you know or know of is interested, first see if you can turn up prospects through any professional associations or business groups you belong to. Once you have rounded up all the usual suspects and discovered that no one is ready to buy, it's probably a good idea to get in touch with a business broker. Ask friends and professional colleagues for their recommendations, and if no one can help, turn to the Yellow Pages listing of business brokers. If you have some to choose from, talk with a few before you make a decision. Look for someone who might have brokered deals for other consultants, or at least can claim some knowledge of the field and how to interest a prospect in a business like yours.

Finding a buyer could take time, so be patient and keep at it. If you or your business broker aren't having any luck in your area, you may have to consider looking elsewhere. If you live in an area that others might like to move to, play this up. You'd be surprised at how many consultants enjoy living in areas where they can drop a hook in a lake at the end of the day, yet find themselves in a big city quickly and easily the next day, working with clients.

Handling the Sale

Let's assume that you have turned up a few prospects. Chances are that this won't turn into a bidding war, so it's unlikely that you will be able to "auction" your business to the highest bidder. The most likely scenario will probably include people you would like to see get the business, and maybe even some you would prefer not to sell to.

A consulting business is a very personal one, and after a few years you develop close relationships with your clients. Therefore, you want to see the person who takes over your business as someone who will mesh well with your clients personally—someone who will be able to provide the same quality of service that you have been providing. Okay, yes, it's an ego thing as well. You may be bright and good at your work, but you're not the only bright and hardworking consultant on the block. And it's a rare sale in which all current clients remain with a new owner. Nonetheless, you should strive to find the kind of person that most of your clients will want to work with. This is especially true if your payout will be made over time. Here are a few tips that will help you move the right prospect to make the right offer:

- Try to get a number of offers, even if you know that some might not be your "perfect" replacement.
- Get as much information as you can about each before you get into any serious discussions and negotiations; a key factor will be whether or not each is financially qualified to buy your business.
- Once you have several serious contenders, stay in touch with each regularly. Don't be pushy, and don't give the impression that you are anxious to sell. Just hinting that others are thinking about buying the business is enough to keep the more serious prospects in the game.
- Leave yourself some negotiating room. Try to give on lesser points while holding firm to the price you are asking. A few minor concessions can often make the difference without having to lower your price.
- Whenever you and a potential buyer come to terms on a disputed issue, put it in writing immediately, send it to him or her, and ask for a confirmation. Selling a business is a step-by-step process, and the more issues you can confirm this way, the less likely they are to surface when you are down to the short strokes.

Selling your business is not like selling your car or some tools you don't use anymore. You are selling something very personal. It's a business that you've built, and it's a contact list that is more than just names on paper. Try to keep this perspective and you should be okay.

How to Overcome the One-Person Handicap

Put yourself in the position of potential buyers for your business. They see what you have done and are impressed. Your prospects may have even met some of your clients and discovered the respect they have for you. And here the prospects are, ready to pay you for your business and to step into your shoes. The nagging question is whether or not they will be able to do what you have done and live up to the image the clients have of you. How can you convince your clients that everything will be okay?

Unless you absolutely must leave the business, the best way to deal with this is not to announce an outright sale, but to announce that you have taken on a full partner. If you have to say something more, simply say that you just want to lighten your workload. Don't announce any planned departure date you may have arranged with the buyer. Sure, some of your clients will sense the deception, and you may have to allude to the fact that your participation will be diminishing. But you can also tell them that you are doing this because you want to make sure that your clients will be well served when—and if—you decide to leave altogether.

This will not only go a long way toward assuring your clients of continued good service, but it will also reduce the fears your buyers may have about who might leave the fold later on. You will have to make good on these promises, but most consultants I have known who have sold their businesses have done this willingly. Few really wanted to quit, but most saw the need for retirement for one reason or another. FYI, I sold my business nine years ago, and I'm still in regular (albeit less frequent) contact with many of my clients who have remained with the person who now owns and runs my former business. Just be sure you keep these contacts as friends, and don't interfere with the business that is now owned by someone else.

1. *A larger consulting firm has offered to buy my business, but a condition of the sale is that I take a staff job with them and manage the clients I bring with me. This is fine, but they also want to base the payout on the retention of the clients. Is this a reasonable proposition?*

    A clean deal is always better than a conditional one. Asking you to stay with the company to ensure a smooth transition is entirely reasonable. However, basing the payout on your ability to retain clients is unreasonable, unless the penalty for any client loss is small. Remember that for any point given in a negotiation, a point should be gained. For example, you might suggest that the payout schedule be heavily weighted on the front end so that any loss would have minimal impact on any client loss. But before you suggest any alternatives, do your best to hold out for a clean deal.

2. *Is it reasonable to allow a prospective buyer for my business to talk with my present clients?*

    If your clients already know that you are planning to sell the business, it's probably a reasonable request. Otherwise, you could jeopardize the value of the business if the prospect fails to make an acceptable offer.

3. *The person who wants to buy my business wants to continue to operate it from my home office, which is a small detached building. He is not willing to pay rent, however. How can I solve this?*

    This may seem far-fetched, but if it's small enough, about the size of a single-car garage, offer to sell it or give it to him if he will pay to have it moved to his own property. Let him make monthly payments to cover the sale. Also, consider letting him use it for a stipulated time, after which he has to move out.

Appendix A

Educational Requirements and Sources

Most consultants never take a course in a subject called "consulting." However, they have had extensive training and experience with the subject on which they consult. There are many distance-learning courses advertised on the Internet that might be of some help. I suggest that you check them out, but don't jump at any of them until you have determined exactly what you feel you need to know in order to practice your profession effectively. You will probably discover that your work experience has already qualified you as an expert in the field in which you want to consult. You will also discover that you might need to improve your support skills, and these usually include financial management, sales and marketing, and the nuts and bolts of running a small business.

Once you have a handle on your needs, check out either distance-learning programs that address these subjects directly, or enroll in any of the continuing education programs that might be offered by local schools, community colleges, and colleges and universities with appropriate programs and courses.

Many colleges and universities also offer courses and programs in specific areas of consulting. For example, Ball State University offers a Certified Training Consultant program based on a series of six three-hour seminars. Those completing the course are entitled to use the designation of Certified Training Consultant (CTC). You can check out this program at bsu.edu/cor/ctc/.

Many professional associations and organizations now work with colleges and universities on subject-specific consulting training programs. Check with any of the associations you belong to in order to see what might be available in your field.

Appendix B

Organizations

There are organizations of consultants in just about every field, and in the more popular fields, there are many different specialized organizations. It would be impossible to list all of them, but to give you an idea of what you might expect from some of the organizations, check out these examples:

- Association of Professional Consultants (http://consultapc.org)
- Society of Professional Consultants (http://spconsultants.org)
- International Guild of Professional Consultants (http://igpc)
- Independent Human Resource Consultants Association (www.ihrca.com)

The best source, and it's enormous, is the Gale Research Directory of Consultants (www.gale.cengage.com). It's available both online and in print. Both are expensive, but most larger libraries with comprehensive reference sections will have copies.

Some of the larger organizations offer training themselves, and some have relationships with schools and universities to provide the specialized training that might be needed to enter specific fields.

Appendix C

Frequently Asked Questions

These questions are typical of the questions asked by people who have attended seminars on starting a consulting business. Unless I miss my guess, you'll find a few of them on the list you already have in mind. I hope the answers will help put you on track.

I have no consulting experience, but I am an expert in my field. How can I turn that experience into a viable consulting business?

If you are currently employed and in no rush to start your own consulting business, the best way to start building a name for yourself is by writing articles for publications that are read by the people you would consider to be prime prospects for business once you get started. If the articles you consider writing can benefit from input from others, consider interviewing those who might be good prospects for your consulting business. Once launched, contact these people to pitch your services. And, of course, use reprints of the articles in your pitches and presentations.

Are any types of articles more beneficial than others in terms of the personal exposure they may produce?

Survey-type articles will put you in touch with the most people. Review the issues that are especially important to those you would consider to be good prospects for the services you plan to offer, as well as good sources of information for your survey article. If you conduct personal interviews, you are in a perfect position to not only make a good impression, but also to learn more about your prospective clients. Be sure to circulate reprints of your articles to all those you plan to contact after you launch your business.

The field I plan to consult in, management assessment, is pretty crowded these days. What would be the best way to enter what is already a competitive field?

There are a number of ways to do this. You might consider starting as a subcontractor for one of the larger consulting firms. It's not uncommon for larger firms to sub out work that would be too costly to staff up for. If there is a niche that the others have either not discovered or have avoided, think about setting out to own that niche. However, be sure you know why it's not covered or possibly even avoided by well-established consultants. Sometimes being the person who takes the plunge into a difficult area gets you some good attention.

My employer has suggested that I start a consulting business with him as my first client. I don't know whether he's trying to tell me that my job is going to evaporate or that he is genuinely interested in seeing me start my own business. Is there any way I can find out without rocking the boat?

Chances are that something is in the wind, so don't be too concerned about rocking the boat. Be up front and ask. If starting a consulting business is already in your plans, this is a gift to accept. See if you can arrange for some continuance of your insurance and retirements plans with your present employer. It's always better to open a new business with some work in hand. You might want to ask your current boss if he or she would be willing to recommend your services to others.

Just how important is it to have a business address other than a home address?

A home office address seldom carries the stigma most newcomers think it will; in fact, you will probably discover that some of the people you consult with are actually envious of your being able to operate from a home office. The important point to remember is to never apologize for operating from a home office. It just isn't necessary. A good consultant's strength is his or her ability to do what is promised. Of course, if you are planning to expand sooner or later, you will probably need more space than might be available in a home office. But, if you expand by using strategic alliances, you may be able to build a large business that can still be managed from a single home office. If your business is such that clients will often be coming to your office, you can make use of one of the many temporary office services that are available in most business centers across the country.

How far ahead should I plan?

Good planning means that you have to cover expenses today, have a solid plan for the first year or two, and a fairly good idea of where you want to be in five or even ten years. Needless to say, your start-up and first year should be planned in fine detail, and you should be able to run the business even if some of the plans don't work out and you have to operate on invested capital. This is one of the reasons for good planning long before you take the plunge. When you know what you are doing and where you want to go, you will be a lot better off than if you were to make the move impulsively.

Just how much of my home expenses can I write off on taxes?

Here's where a lot of new, home-based consultants get into a lot of trouble. The tax rules are very specific, and unless you follow them exactly, you could be the target of a tax audit. And that can be an expensive nightmare. Many people who are audited start out by obeying the rules; then, they gradually start relaxing the way they interpret them until they reach the tipping point. Read the chapter on taxes, get advice from your accountant, and do what you are told!

I need start-up capital, but most banks I've talked with aren't interested in lending money to a home-based consultant. Where can I get the start-up money I need?

The banks you talked with aren't interested mainly because a consulting business has little or no collateral to put up to secure the loan. If you have paid off a significant portion of a mortgage, they might be interested. Most home-based consultancies are launched with personal savings, loans from friends and relatives, and stock purchase (if the company is incorporated). But from an investment perspective, stock in a corporation that has no assets is not very different from an individual loan to start out as a sole proprietary. In fact, it can be even riskier for investors if the corporation runs up debt and has to close its doors. The stockholders can be held liable for a portion of the debt. All this argues for careful advance planning and setting aside the finds that will be needed. You may have to cut back on some of your expenses early on, but when you cross the line into profitability, it will be yours—all yours!

I've been told that a limited liability corporation is the best way to establish a home-based consulting business. Is this the route I should take?

The answer is a resounding yes—and no! There are far too many variables in the start-up of every business to say flat out that an LLC is the best way for you to go. Most people are very interested in the protection the corporate forms offer, but until you know exactly where you might be vulnerable, do not make an automatic decision to go with an LLC. The extra personal protection an LLC offers over a conventional corporation can vanish if the trouble you find yourself in is a result of your acting illegally, unethically, or irresponsibly. The tax advantages and disadvantages are probably more important than the protections either form offers. Check with an attorney before you make a decision.

I am thinking about buying an existing and successful one-person consulting business. What are the benefits and pitfalls of doing this?

The major benefit is that you will have income the moment you open the door. There might be significant accounts receivable–based contracts the owner has made that you will have to fulfill. The main drawback is that you are not the person who has built the reputation of the business, and unless you can convince the existing clients that you are as good—or better—than the person they have been dealing with, the clients will be fair game for other consultants until you can prove yourself. The best move in this case is for you to become a "partner" in the business for a long-enough period prior to your purchase, so that the clients can get to know you before the owner bows out for good. Most consultants who sell their businesses this way report that they do not introduce the "partner" as the future owner, but as someone they have taken on to "grow the business." This projects a dynamic image of the firm rather than a picture of potential instability.

Index

Twelve Angry Men (film), 59

V
visualization exercises, 18–22

W
Web sites, 141–42
Weinstein, Grace W., 46, 77, 88, 102
workload, 22–23

Z
Zappa, Frank, 107

About the Author

Bert Holtje founded James Peter Associates, Inc. in 1970. The firm served as an independent book producer and literary agency, and provided consulting, editorial, and promotional services until it was sold in 2000. JPA represented eighty-seven authors of nonfiction books and placed over six hundred books with major U.S. and world publishers. It also provided extensive direct marketing services to Prentice-Hall, McGraw-Hill, and other book publishers. Bert Holtje is the author of eleven books published by major publishers under his own name and more than twenty others as the collaborator or ghostwriter. He has BS and MA degrees in psychology and marketing. His editorial interests include business, psychology, self-help, science, technology, history, and politics. Bert now provides consulting services to authors, agents, and publishers which include ghostwriting, proposal development, manuscript development, and collaboration. He lives in Tenafly, New Jersey.